THE TAINTED TRIAL OF FARAH JAMA

THE TAINTED TRIAL OF FARAH JAMA

JULIE SZEGO

Published by Wild Dingo Press
Melbourne, Australia
books@wilddingopress.com.au
www.wilddingopress.com.au

First published by Wild Dingo Press 2014.

Text copyright © Julie Szego

The moral right of the author has been asserted.

Except as permitted under the Australian Copyright Act 1968,
no part of this book may be reproduced, stored in a retrieval system,
or transmitted in any form or by any means, electronic, mechanical,
photocopying, recording, or otherwise without prior permission
of the copyright owner and the publisher of this book.

Cover and internal design: Susan Miller, millervision@netspace.net.au
Editor: Katia Ariel and Iris Breuer
Printed in Australia by Ligare

National Library in Australia
Cataloguing-in-Publications Data
Szego, Julie, 1969–
The tainted trial of Farah Jama / Julie Szego.

ISBN: 9780987381149 (paperback)

Jama, Farah Abdulkadir.
Boden, Kimani.
Sonnet, Brett.
Rape–Victoria–Investigation.
DNA fingerprinting–Victoria.
Evidence tampering–Victoria.
Forensic pathology–Victoria.
Judicial error–Victoria.

363.2509945

Only sustainably grown wood is used for the manufacture
of paper in this book.

Julie Szego began her career as a lawyer before she switched to journalism. She spent 12 years at *The Age* newspaper where she held various roles, including social affairs reporter, senior writer, leader writer and fortnightly columnist. During her time at the paper she wrote a number of highly-acclaimed pieces to mark the 60th anniversary of the liberation of Auschwitz, investigated the cultural divide between the inner-city and the outer suburbs as part of an award-winning series on Melbourne, and wrote a profile of the Somali-Dutch-American feminist activist, Ayaan Hirsi Ali.

She wrote a monthly column for *The Australian Jewish News* for seven years, contributed to a book of essays on Australian Jewish culture and edited and interpreted her father's 2001 memoir, *Two Prayers to One God*. She also teaches university courses in writing and journalism. *The Tainted Trial of Farah Jama* is her first book.

Disclaimer

The utmost care has been taken to accurately record and represent the people and events in this story. Some names and details have been changed to protect their identity or privacy.

The publishers assume no legal liability or responsibility for unintended inaccuracies, but would be pleased to rectify at the earliest opportunity any omissions or errors brought to their notice.

Acknowledgements

This book owes its existence to my former *Age* colleague Liz Porter, whose award-winning feature on the Farah Jama case led to an approach from Wild Dingo Press, which, through a fortuitous chain of events, not least a recommendation from my dear friend and mentor Karen Kissane, led to an approach to me. I am further indebted to Liz for her generosity with documents and contacts, and her invaluable and prompt advice.

That the narrative took shape at all is thanks in no small part to the tough love and unwavering support of Michael Gawenda, the unfailing patience and intellectual rigour of my sister Klara and the masterful insight and immense talent of my editor, Katia Ariel. The sweetest gift of all came from Helen Garner, who sets the standard to which all non-fiction writers ought to aspire. Her breathtaking generosity and down-to-earth friendship not only enhanced the book but also enriched my life.

At Wild Dingo Press, Iris Breuer executed a thorough final edit, my research assistant and occasional agent-in-espionage, Jessica Carrascalão Heard never said no and neither did my warm-hearted and inspirational publisher Cathi Lewis, who kept me strong throughout. Writers Victoria provided a studio-of-one's-own at historic Glenfern, Marcella Paska assisted with baby-sitting and a first draft was born.

I'm deeply grateful to the following friends and experts for their contributions to *The Tainted Trial*: Aggie Vlahos, Zohar Berchik, Anna Davey, Dr David Dorward, Graham Reilly, Dick Gross, Jane Taupin, Professor Ross Coppel, Natalia Coppel, Peter Chadwick SC, Patrick Tehan QC, Associate Professor Jeremy Gans, Mizz De Zoysa-Lewis, Nic Pullen.

To my children Sara and Hannah and my father George, I can only say thank you, for everything. It is also all I can say to my late mother Eva, who is with me every moment of every day and whose no-nonsense endorsement of the manuscript will stand as the most affirming of all reviews.

And finally to my partner, Tony. I dedicate this book to him, and I reckon that says it all.

Chapter 1

'Pull up her pants.'

It was a female voice. And then somewhere a male voice. Maria sensed three or four people huddled round her. It was dark, she was lying on her back and her pants were down.

A blurred panic, a rush of vertigo, a sinking terror. The floor caving in beneath her. An ache in her eyes. Her head, heavy as a brick, in someone's lap, the woman's voice closer than before.

'What's your name?'

'What time did you get here tonight?'

Now something was covering her body. A blanket? Maria felt intense pain in her armpits, her chest and over her sternum. A wave of nausea washed over her. She could smell vomit.

The scandal of Farah Jama, the Somali teenager accused of raping Maria, must start here, with the woman nearly thirty years his senior.

The week leading up to the calamitous night of 15 July 2006 had been a tough one for Maria. Work was demanding and her relationship was slowly dying. Keen to unwind, she rang her friend, Sophie, to suggest they go out on the weekend. The women decided on a mature-age nightclub that catered for people twenty-eight and over, in Doncaster in Melbourne's east. In the early evening on Saturday, Maria ate a light meal. She then dressed for the night: black stretch pants with a zip in the front, a top with spaghetti straps, a cropped cardigan with sequins, a coat with fur around the collar and cuffs, a silver handbag and no underwear.

She brushed her shoulder-length hair so that it fell in a gentle curve against one side of her face. At about 8.30 pm Sophie arrived with her partner, Alex, to pick her up. Maria climbed into the car carrying her handbag and a large, unopened bottle of the hazelnut liqueur Frangelico, the only alcoholic drink she really liked. The trio headed out to Doncaster in good spirits.

Alex turned off Williamsons Road, opposite the monolith of the Westfield shopping complex. He pulled into a spot near the entrance to the aptly-named Venue 28 nightclub, the women staying in the car while he bought tickets from the venue office. By the time he returned, Maria had nearly downed her first drink of Frangelico from tumbler-sized plastic glasses that Sophie had brought from home. Sophie preferred Southern-Comfort-and-Coke and came equipped with a bottle of her own. Maria drank another, or possibly another two, Frangelicos. The drinks inside the club were a bloody rip-off, after all, and nattering in the car was fun.

They turned on the radio. For more than an hour, the friends drank and chatted in the car, before they finally went in.

The security footage of the entrance to Venue 28 captured the trio's arrival at 10.20 pm.

Sophie and Alex rushed to the dance floor. Maria wouldn't see the couple again for the rest of the night, and once the night was done she wouldn't want to see them at all. Finding herself suddenly alone, Maria tried to look purposeful. She checked her jacket at the cloakroom near the entrance, visited the toilet and walked the carpeted floor to the closest of the club's three bars.

'Frangelico with ice,' she told the male bartender. He poured her a single shot in a tumbler-sized glass.

Drink in hand, she ambled over to one of the chest-high standing tables, put down her glass and lit a cigarette. For a few minutes she sipped her drink and smoked, then strolled to the lounge area, where she smoked some more. At one point she went in search of Sophie and Alex, trying to find them on the expansive dance floor that scooped from one end of the club to the other in the shape of a giant grin. But the place was too packed, so she gave up.

She was making her way to another of the club's bars when a youthful, dark-haired man struck up a conversation. He was with some other men and gave his name as Stefan. For a few minutes Maria made small talk, half-heartedly. She then returned to the bar to order another Frangelico with ice. This was her fourth, maybe fifth, drink in less than two hours.

Again, she wandered aimlessly about, then stopped at another round standing table, alongside a pillar. She rested her glass on the table so she could take her pack of cigarettes and lighter out of her handbag. Again, she smoked and sipped her drink.

This time two men approached and struck up a conversation. They were olive-skinned and of southern European background. One was tall, with dark, wavy brown hair. He wore a white shirt. He wasted no time telling Maria that he had a girlfriend. The other man was shorter and seemed older than his companion, mid- to late-thirties perhaps. He was dark-haired and unshaven. Again for only a few minutes, Maria chatted with the men. She chatted about the soccer, chatted about nothing in particular.

But she took an instant dislike to the shorter man. He seemed an intense, pushy type. And as she would tell police, she certainly 'wasn't there to pick up or meet anyone'. That short bloke is a bit sleazy, she thought. She began to have a bad feeling about him.

And then darkness.

⋈⋈

On 14 July 2008, a young Somali man stood trial in the County Court of Victoria for the rape of a forty-eight year old woman while she was unconscious at a Doncaster nightclub. The man, twenty-one year old Farah Abdulkadir Jama of Preston, pleaded not guilty to the crime. The jurors saw in the dock an athletic-looking African youth with strong features. Eyebrows raised, head tilted slightly back, he appeared dismissive and defiant.

He appeared defiant even as the Crown led DNA evidence of Jama having had sex with the woman without her consent. Samples taken from the woman's body were found to contain DNA from a male, and a routine check of the police database established that male to be Jama. It was the only evidence the Crown had against the youth, but it was nevertheless devastating. In the prosecutor's words, the evidence was 'rock solid'.

Jama said he had never even seen the woman before, and raised an alibi in his defence. Witnesses called on Jama's behalf claimed the youth had spent the night in question with his family, at the bedside of his gravely ill father, reciting the Koran.

Nonetheless, the trial was regarded by the judge and the barristers as a relatively straightforward affair, save for one complication, one rather delicate problem. It arose when the jury tackled the elephant in the room and asked what the judge, in their absence, described as the 'inevitable' question. How had Jama's DNA profile come to be on the police database in the first place? In other words, why was the young man known to police at all? But the judge, constrained by the rules of evidence under which prejudicial information is withheld from the jury, gave the 'inevitable' question short shrift. The answer was irrelevant, he told the jurors, and they were 'not to speculate' about it.

After a five-day trial, which attracted media interest, the jury found the accused guilty as charged. At the sentencing hearing, held after the verdict, defence counsel asked the judge to take into account Jama's age, only nineteen at the time of the offence; his close ties with family and community; and his traumatic childhood as a refugee from civil war. The judge weighed these factors against the youth's lack of remorse, the victim's considerable suffering and the thoroughly 'reprehensible' nature of the crime, to pronounce a gaol term of six years, with a non-parole minimum of four.

The next time Farah Jama made headlines was on Monday 7 December 2009, nearly a year and a half after his conviction. Only now, on the steps of the Court of Appeal, the microphones were tuned to catch his words, the TV cameras rolled as he posed triumphant, his arm around the shoulders of his new lawyer, a man with brown skin, high forehead and telegenic grin. Jama's light grey jacket had come off, his tie askew, lilac shirt freed from suit pants.

The lawyer hailed a momentous day for his client. After sixteen months in custody, he was cleared of all charges. The Court of Appeal had been persuaded that Jama suffered a wrongful conviction, his case a substantial miscarriage of justice, the 'rock-solid' evidence against him reduced to rubble. Photographers snapped the innocent man, euphoric in his vindication. Some shots taken that morning capture Jama weary and overwhelmed; eyelids heavy, head in an awkward twist away from his body. In another, he's staring at a point above the ground, a joyous smile cresting on his face, as if he has just grasped the unequivocal nature of his victory.

By the time I got wind of the controversy it was already yesterday's news. I read a report in *The Age* before I dressed for work, brain grinding into gear. My gaze lingered on the photo of Jama and his lawyer. I felt a twinge of discomfort, mingled with curiosity. A black kid. Did that have anything to do with it? I abruptly muffled the thought. It was uncharacteristic, and it made me uncomfortable. I believe in 'The System'; I'm that kind of person. I reflexively attribute errors in the dispensation of justice to cock-up rather than conspiracy. Such instances are sad and regrettable and always impart a lesson, but, alas, *these things happen*.

My drowsy reasoning was right to a degree: no cunning plan had been hatched by authorities to put a young African man behind bars for a crime he didn't commit. But I would come to realise that one of the most confounding, most chilling, aspects of the trial of Farah Jama was that most of the criminal justice professionals in his case had acted in good faith, without even the vaguest hint of malice.

Still, on that morning I already felt a tug from the story's undertow. So, when more than a year later a publisher approached me, on a colleague's recommendation, to write the Farah Jama story, I cheerfully agreed, figuring I could tell the tale from a pedestal of journalistic detachment, delivering judgment from on high.

I figured wrong. In fact, I was doomed to pass judgment on myself, with the verdict less than flattering.

Chapter 2

Stephanie Johnstone, nightclub supervisor, had been doing laps around the venue, picking up glasses and plates, issuing orders to staff, when at 10.50 pm a security guard approached her. There was a problem in the female toilets near Bar Three and the DJ booth, he said. Johnstone went to check it out.

Walking into the toilet block, she saw a woman's leg poking out beneath the door of the first cubicle on the left. There was no sound from inside. Johnstone bent down. In the gap between the door and the floor she could see the woman sitting motionless on the floor. She tried to push open the cubicle door, but it was locked. She tried speaking to the woman, but there was no response. So Johnstone went into the adjoining cubicle, climbed onto the toilet seat and stepped on the sanitary napkin disposal unit. Springing up on her toes, she peered over the other side. The woman was slumped at an angle, her back against the wall and door, the button and zip of her pants undone.

Immediately, Johnstone hoisted herself over the wall and into the cubicle where she grabbed hold of the woman and tried unsuccessfully to drag her away from the door.

'I need to get someone out of the toilets,' Johnstone yelled to a guard outside. A female patron arrived and also climbed over the wall. The two grasped firmly under the woman's arm and managed to slide her across the floor away from the door, so that it could be opened. Johnstone called out to three security guards who had been waiting outside the toilets. They rushed in and hauled the woman up, one on either side holding under her armpits, the third grabbing each ankle. Johnstone picked up the woman's handbag and followed.

The men lumbered down past the DJ booth and along the dance floor, backtracking and shifting course to avoid bumping into patrons. They carried the unconscious woman up three lots of stairs to the band room in the backstage area. At one point the guard holding the woman's feet lost his grip and a heel thumped to the floor. The band room, its carpet criss-crossed with silvery duct tape to hold down cords, was virtually the only part of the club that offered some calm and privacy. The guards laid the woman down on her side. By this time, her pants had slipped down to her hips.

Johnstone sent another employee to ring for an ambulance. The woman was regaining consciousness. She seemed confused and fearful, intimidated by the crowd surrounding her. Johnstone was kneeling with the woman's head on her lap. 'What's your name?' she asked. No response. Someone covered the woman with a curtain.

'Are you allergic to penicillin?'

Johnstone persisted: Who was she here with? Had she been drinking? Did she know how long she'd spent on the floor of the toilet cubicle?

The woman looked dazed. Johnstone repeated several of the questions.

'What time did you get here tonight?'

'What time is it now?' the woman responded.

Johnstone gave her some water. The woman murmured, over and over, 'I'm sorry'.

'You have nothing to be sorry about.' Johnstone tried her best to soothe the woman whose name she now knew as Maria, stroking her head as it rested on her knees.

Maria said she felt sick and was going to throw up. One of the security guards, Mikayil Umar, urged her to vomit.

'Just let it out,' he said. 'You're okay here, just let it out.'

In the ambulance a female paramedic asked Maria more questions, but she could only repeat, 'I'm sorry. I just don't know what happened'.

At about 12.30 am the ambulance pulled in at the Emergency Department of the Austin Hospital at Heidelberg, in the city's northeast. The triage nurses at reception saw a middle-aged woman brought in on a stretcher. They were told she had been found unconscious on the floor of a nightclub toilet cubicle; hardly an unusual scenario on a Saturday night in Melbourne. But this woman seemed worse than the norm. She was unresponsive, vomiting over and over. The nurses swiftly moved her into a resuscitation bay.

Doctors and nurses seemed to be swirling round and over her. A battery of tests, muttered suspicion. Maria felt something stuck to her buttock.

'You've got tape on your bottom,' a nurse said, ripping the black strips from her skin.

Chapter 3

'How are you gonna start this book? Where you gonna start it?' Jama asked, arching his eyebrows and tilting his head back in his signature expression which, depending on the context, could be read as either quizzical or contrary.

We were in the publisher's office in Windsor. Jama had arrived about forty minutes late, navigating his way from Preston with the help of a GPS. It was April 2011, about fifteen months since the Court of Appeal cleared his name. We sat on opposite sides of a wide conference table, stealing glances at one another, as if this were a first date or, more fittingly, an arranged marriage.

I felt taken aback by the question and the look.

'Oh I can't answer that question yet,' I said, 'that'll only come much later once my research is done.'

In more than a decade in journalism, I had never heard an interview subject ask such a technical question. Was Jama the overbearing, micro-managing type, I thought with fleeting anxiety.

Jama had spoken publicly of his wish to write a book about his ordeal, 'as a kind of therapy'. He wanted people to know precisely what was done to him. He wanted to pose the question 'Is this fair?' Still, the publisher wanted an independent person to write a book based on the events; someone prepared to work closely with Jama without ghosting his narrative. She already sensed his unmediated account could raise problems. She told me how at the conclusion of a previous meeting with Jama and his all-male entourage of lawyers and relatives, he was set to launch into an earnest dissertation about gender relations.

'You see,' he began, 'the problem with this country is that women have too much power—'

The older, and savvier, men in the room cut him off.

So I had been explaining to Jama what the process of our working together would entail: he and I would be spending lots of time together; I would also need to speak with his family; I would be asking many questions, some of them awkward. I stressed he may not like everything I would write. The best books, I explained, drew vivid portraits of people, with all their strengths and flaws.

Jama nodded, murmuring, 'Yeah,' 'OK', 'Yep', 'That's fine.' From the beginning, my impression was of a basically likeable person, and it would remain so notwithstanding the unpleasantness ahead. While I started at his question about beginnings, some months later I wondered if Jama had intended it more literally. Maybe he wasn't asking about my narrative technique, but simply wanted to know where the story would start in terms of chronology. Perhaps he had a view about where he did *not* want the story to start. In any event, the prickly moment passed. Jama and I locked eyes and he smiled—a brilliant, sweet and shy smile. *He's still just a boy.* I felt a surge of maternal tenderness. But at some point after this meeting Jama's enthusiasm for the book began to sour.

A month later, on the last day of May, I rang him to suggest we meet for coffee; a getting-to-know-you session, no pressure. Jama agreed, but he seemed wary. He made a point of telling me that he was still making his mind up about whether to sign a contract. I had been eager to visit him at home in Preston, but Jama proposed meeting at a cafe on Lygon Street, Carlton.

He arrived wearing sunglasses, jeans and a dark jacket of light wool with a white border. It had a decorative feature, resembling an unfolding handkerchief or a black rose at the breast pocket. This time, one-on-one, Jama seemed older and more confident. I even detected a slight swagger; inevitable, perhaps, when a twenty-three-year-old, still living at home, suddenly has half a million dollars in his pocket—the payment he had received a year earlier as compensation for his wrongful conviction. On this occasion, though, I was not to see his brilliant, bashful smile.

I lobbed some broad questions. What was he doing with himself? Had he been going out? Who was he hanging out with these days?

He explained that since his release from gaol about eighteen months earlier he had been brushing up on physics and maths. He was preparing for an entrance exam in November, for a course in aircraft maintenance engineering.

Sometimes he slept in and studied in the afternoon. He had four or five close friends, all Somalis, who were either finishing off their studies or working; one was interstate. He also had heaps of other friends from around the neighbourhood. He reeled off a list of nationalities. For some reason the only one I jotted down was 'Serbs'.

Jama kept his answers short, his eyes restless and wandering.

'Did you enjoy high school?' I asked.

He rolled his eyes and shifted in his seat. 'I'm not going to talk about these personal things.'

'What was the problem with high school?'

'There was no problem,' he sighed, wriggling again. 'High school was fine. But there were some issues … Look, believe me, I could tell you things that would blow your mind, but not *now*.'

He reminded me that he had still not agreed to the book. He veered onto the subject of film rights. It dawned on me that he cared little about a book. What he really wanted was a movie of his experiences. I was beginning to feel a tension between the story he was expecting and the one I needed to pursue. Suddenly he leaned forward.

'You want to write this for your career, yes?' His tone was sneering. 'You want me to give up everything that's in my head, everything I went through *inside*.'

I steered the conversation towards the broader themes that emerged from his story.

'Men and women, racism, sexual assault, African communities …' I trailed off at '… even Islam.'

Jama's eyes had long glazed over, but these words jolted him. 'Nuh!' He jerked his frame back in the chair. 'Oh, that's too political! It has nothing to do with Islam.'

'But of course it has to do with Islam. The alibi witnesses at the trial said that on the night in question you were at your father's bedside, reciting the Koran. And the jury obviously didn't believe them.'

'Well okay,' he said, 'I guess that's kind of about Islam.'

He asked if I would work for him, help him write his own story. I declined, saying that as a journalist I wouldn't feel right about that.

He listened, and in that moment seemed mature and restrained and dignified.

I began to talk about his family history, how powerful a story it was. By this stage I had read an article about his case, written the previous year by my then *Age* colleague, Liz Porter. The piece included an interview with Jama, who briefly described some key moments in his ordeal, and basic information about his background. So I knew something of his family's escape from civil war, starting afresh, making something of their lives. I talked about his mother, who had believed in him all along and wouldn't rest until the truth came out.

'Yeah, she was amazing,' he mumbled, fidgeting, eyes darting round the room as if checking for emergency exits.

Then he spoke firmly and abruptly. 'That's it for now.'

Against my wishes and expectations, he insisted on picking up the tab.

A few days later, we talked at length on the phone. I told Jama I was eager to make a time to get started on interviews. Jama made it clear that he still hadn't signed a contract. He was holding on to the rights to his story and how it would be told. Anticipating the hard slog that lay ahead, I also argued for what I regarded as my fair share of rights and royalties.

At this point, I most likely sealed my fate by suggesting I could, if push came to shove, write the book without him. I was beginning to see beyond him to the story. I was beginning, in fact, to come round to the view that his involvement might actually hinder me from understanding how on earth so appalling an injustice could happen in Melbourne in these times. Perhaps he would seek to restrict my perspective when the sorry tale needed to be seen in wide-angle as well as in close-up.

His voice dropped an octave. 'Okay, I'm just trying to be a good person here. Without me, you have nothing.'

From there on, things moved swiftly to crisis point. The publisher set a deadline for him to agree to the book. The deadline came and went in silence. My Somali friend, Yusuf Omar, offered some gentle advice about the tortured negotiations and unmet deadline, 'There's something you have to know about us Somalis; we come from a nomadic culture.' I cut him off, impatient with where I knew he was going: Somalis and nomads and culturally-determined ideas about times and dates. But this wasn't about my Western rationality bucking against a mythical Africa, in which the vast, windswept and disorienting savannah makes a mockery of things such as deadlines. Jama knew the deal and had ditched it.

The immensity of the task that lay ahead was finally beginning to dawn on me. I already sensed the saga could not be fully understood without some knowledge of the once accused, of the complex and sometimes secretive culture he springs from, and the radically different worlds he must negotiate.

As for Jama and me, we did meet one last time.

I had met with some leaders from Melbourne's Somali community while researching a feature article in 2006. I remember a group of men, polite if somewhat guarded, anxious to elaborate on the challenges that faced Horn of Africa refugees in their new land. One of those men was Abdurahman Osman, who would give evidence at Jama's sentencing hearing both as the youth's paternal uncle and as president of the Somali Association of Victoria.

About three months after the collapse of negotiations with Jama, I phoned Osman thinking it was worth a shot. I chirped about our having met years ago. He didn't remember? Oh well, he'd probably recognise me if he saw me. And, well, I would like to see him because perhaps he wasn't aware, but I was writing the story of his nephew, Farah Jama. And perhaps he wasn't aware that Jama had at one stage been involved in contractual negotiations with me. Perhaps Jama was writing his own book, I said, and why not? But given I was also writing a book, well, it would be a good idea if we talked.

Osman interrupted. 'No, no, we don't let him write this

book! We are his family and we don't let him write it: we tell him, we don't want two books, three books. There must be just one book! I'll speak to him,' Osman assured me.

He asked me to meet him at his restaurant in Flemington on Saturday. It being Ramadan, customers would be few, and we could talk freely. The conversation felt like a win, despite my niggling sense of wires being crossed.

On Saturday I set out in good time. I recognised the neighbourhood as the epicentre of Somali Melbourne, particularly the public housing towers in which the authorities bunched the new arrivals in the 1990s. Osman, according to his evidence at Jama's sentencing hearing, was also living there, running the community group from the premises. For some years an abandoned warehouse opposite the towers on Boundary Road, known as 'The Eight Blacks', after a former Aboriginal meeting place on the site, had functioned as a pool-hall-cum-cafe, with a makeshift prayer room upstairs. It was revealed in 2009 that the place had come under Federal Police and ASIO surveillance as an after-hours' fundraising and recruitment hub for militant Islamists.

The restaurant was a casual and sparsely-furnished eatery wedged between two cafés on Racecourse Road. Osman muttered a greeting as he opened the door. I caught a glimpse of a veiled woman, who swiftly disappeared out the back. A cherubic little boy played on a laptop at one of the tables. I then saw the muscular back of a man in a bomber jacket near the counter. Jama. Although I should have seen it coming, I felt rattled—which was, of course, the point. His presence constituted an ambush.

Osman and I faced one another across a table. He appeared in his mid-sixties, fairly lean and slightly scruffy, with wavy grey hair and cloudy, blue-green eyes. From a recent radio interview, I knew he regularly chewed khat, a leaf with amphetamine-like effects. I also remembered from the court transcript of the sentencing hearing that before Osman had given evidence, Jama's counsel told the judge, 'I don't wish to embarrass Mr Osman, but when you see him in the witness box you will notice a scar on his head and on his nose. He said that he was put into a political prison there in Somalia and beaten and tortured and hit on the head with an axe in gaol—he's lucky to be alive. That might give you some idea of what these people faced …'

That scar appeared as a thin line, sloping towards the ridge of his nose.

Osman gave every impression of a man who liked running things. At trial he had mentioned having held leadership positions in two refugee camps in Kenya in the early 1990s; he was a section 'head' in one camp, and the 'vice chairperson' of the other. His use of the politically-correct 'chairperson' jarred as I questioned the likelihood of a Somali woman being made leader of a refugee camp.

Jama swept round and slid into the chair next to his uncle. He placed his clenched palms on the table and stiffened his back inside the bomber jacket.

'Farah, I didn't expect to see you here.' I fussed with my bag as he glowered in my direction. 'But it's always a pleasure.'

His face, tight with rage, looked handsome.

'I have spoken to Farah,' Osman began, 'and it seems that

the situation is very different from what you told me on the phone. What you said wasn't true.'

I said that I was contracted to write this book, even though Jama had decided not to be involved. Jama retorted that he was writing his own book with an American publisher.

'I don't allow you to write this book,' Jama said. 'I don't authorise you.'

He spoke with a faint blend of several accents, which included a vaguely British-sounding inflection that I later twigged was likely a hangover from the two years he spent in New Zealand before he came to Australia. In his presence I again felt a maternal protectiveness.

I explained that journalists write unauthorised stories about people all the time. Scowling, he pointed his finger at me, 'You'd better not get anything wrong. You better not use my name … better not talk about the history—'

'Quiet, Farah, stop,' Osman interrupted. 'Don't say anything!'

I asked what he meant by 'the history'.

'What I went through in prison,' Jama mumbled.

Osman cut in, also wagging his finger. 'This is HIS story! It happened to him! Only he knows what's true, what really happened!' His finger trembled as his voice climbed. 'What do you know about his history?'

I flinched. He was right. Journalists swoop on other people's stories, pick the eyes out, mangle and reshape until they're something entirely different. We thieve and desecrate for a living.

The confrontation went round in circles. I prattled on

once more about the story being in the public interest, about 'failures across the criminal justice system' and the other two returned, naturally enough, to Jama's interests. Then Osman sought to wind the meeting up.

'We have spoken to lawyers, many lawyers,' he said. 'So okay, we cannot stop you from writing.'

'And if you keep harassing me …' Jama's eyes narrowed. 'Calling my uncle—'

Osman cut him off again. 'Don't say anything, Farah.'

He turned to me. 'Now, we tell you. We! Farah! The family! We will not co-operate with you!'

I said I understood. Osman hurriedly asked if I wanted a drink. 'We won't drink because it is Ramadan and we are fasting, but if you would like a drink I'll make you one.'

I declined the offer.

Back in the car, my fingers shook as I turned on the ignition. My breathing slowed only once I had crossed the Yarra River and edged towards my part of town, where the butchers are typically kosher rather than halal.

'This is HIS story,' Osman had thundered.

But the Farah Jama case was tangled up with the stories of two women. The first was that of Maria, whose inner life careened out of control in the aftermath of the night in Doncaster. The second belonged to a young woman, whose encounter with Jama at a pool hall, on the other side of town, set in motion a freakish train of disasters.

Chapter 4

Dr Christopher Kay, anaesthetic registrar at the Austin hospital, observed with a degree of puzzlement the woman who was lying on the trolley before him in the emergency department. For reasons he couldn't entirely fathom, she was lapsing in and out of consciousness. He listened to her heart and chest. He felt her abdomen, and tapped various parts of her body to test her reflexes. Nothing struck him as unusual.

'Maria!' he said, loudly. She roused, opening her eyes. Kay pressed hard on her fingernail, this time to no avail. 'Unresponsive to painful stimuli,' Kay noted. It was a bad sign for sure, he thought, so bad she perhaps needed a breathing tube to protect her airways. They had better keep a close eye on her.

Kay looked at the results of Maria's blood test taken around one o'clock that morning. It showed, hours after her last drink, a blood alcohol concentration of 0.13, nearly three times the legal driving limit. But this woman seemed even more intoxicated than that. Something wasn't quite right. Perhaps she had consumed an illicit drug of some sort? Best send a urine sample off for a toxicology screening, he decided. If she had taken anything nasty, voluntarily or otherwise, they could find out before her system flushed it away.

Later that morning he returned to check on her. Her blood pressure was low and she had complained of feeling light-headed when she tried to stand. He gave her intravenous fluids to guard against dehydration, and prescribed an anti-nausea drug.

※

Early on Sunday morning Detective Senior Constable Karen Porter, on duty at Doncaster station, received a call about a suspected rape victim under observation at the Austin. She was told the woman had been found unconscious in Venue 28, the nightclub in Doncaster's Hotel Shoppingtown. Following the usual procedure for rape cases, she contacted officers from the Sexual Offences Unit at nearby Diamond Creek police station and arranged to meet up with them at the Austin.

Porter arrived at the hospital before nine. Approaching the suspected victim, the detective found her vague and bewildered. She tried to learn some details about the night before, her only clue so far being some strips of black duct tape that the nurses in emergency said they had found on the woman's behind. After a brief exchange, Porter jotted down some notes. '… *Arrived at about 21:30 hours and sat in car having a few drinks, [friend] drove to the location. M had … approx. 3 x shots from bottle of Frangelico she bought* (sic) *from home.*'

Porter briefed her specialist colleagues from the Sexual Offences Unit as best she could. Perhaps there would be more leads once she had inspected the venue.

Hotel Shoppingtown is a terraced series of buildings comprising a bistro, gaming area and rather faded cabaret room, which hosts the nightclub. Venue 28 being closed on a Sunday, Porter had to gain entry through the kitchen of the downstairs bistro, which was also how staff moved around the place on a busy night. She arranged for the previous night's security footage, which showed patrons coming and going, to be downloaded onto a disk. She would view it carefully back at the station. She took photos of the female toilets near Bar Three, the entrance to the venue, and the backstage area. Noticing a vomit stain and duct tape on the carpet, she snapped them too.

In cases of suspected rape, especially rape by an unknown and seemingly dangerous predator, an entirely separate apparatus of the criminal justice system cranks into gear. Specialists are enlisted fast, and often in significant numbers: duty police and local police—their numbers suddenly doubling with a change of shift—officers from the Sexual Offences and Child Abuse Investigation Teams, investigators from the Sexual Crimes Squad and forensic medical officers. Sometimes there may be close to twenty officials on the scene, with the victim required to tell their story over and over. The professionals have critical roles to perform, and they do so with a sense of urgency, time being of the essence.

But as I learned from a counsellor at the Centres Against Sexual Assault (CASA), a government-funded support and advocacy group, all this activity can overwhelm the victim. So the counsellors see it as their mission to give the woman (the victim almost always being a woman) some space. Their job is to listen and to advise. They guide the victim through her options: notify the police, take the morning-after pill, ask for a medical, all the above, none of the above. Whatever happens next must be the victim's decision alone, that's the most important thing.

And so, on that Sunday, a counsellor from CASA visited Maria for the routine 'options talk', as a result of which Maria opted for a forensic medical examination to ascertain whether her worst fears about the night before had any basis in fact.

In the mid-morning, Dr Nicola Cunningham, a registrar at the Victorian Institute of Forensic Medicine, was paged to the crisis care unit adjacent to the Austin's emergency department. The unit, known as Northern CASA, is one of fifteen administered by the victims' advocacy group in Victoria and its design reflects the overall mission. Victims have their 'options talk' in a counselling room that's rather sparse, with little more than chair, desk and couch, but suitably private. Those who elect for a medical need only go next door to the examination room, another sparse but functional interior consisting of a bed covered with a disposable 'bluey' hospital sheet, an overhead lamp and a metal trolley pre-stocked with microscope slides, scissors and sealed instruments.

Cunningham most likely approached the examination room with a sense of déjà vu. On call throughout the weekend, she had been summoned here, to the same seldom-used room, little more than twenty-four hours before, at about four o'clock in the morning, to attend to another suspected rape victim, a young woman who came accompanied by police officers and a friend. The woman's hair was matted with semen. When Cunningham insisted some strands be cut and bagged for forensics, the young woman had whined in girly protest.

This time Cunningham was confronted with a mature, rather dazed woman wearing a hospital gown over black stretch pants. As is routine, the doctor asked for a brief medical history. The woman described several health problems. Cunningham made notes. *Bipolar*. She jotted this one down too. 'Any allergies?' Cunningham asked.

Maria cited the brand name of a strong pain reliever.

'What happens when you take this drug?' Cunningham queried.

'Brain syndrome,' the patient said.

Could she perhaps explain what that meant? No, Maria could not elaborate.

Brain syndrome, scribbled Cunningham.

The doctor quizzed Maria about her recollections of the night before. She observed bruises on the woman's arms, elbows and armpits, on her chest wall and right breast. Blunt trauma, Cunningham concluded, resulting from a blow, or forceful contact with a blunt object. Maria said the bruises on her forearms were probably old, but she didn't know how the ones on her arms and breast had got there. Cunningham took photographs of the injuries.

Maria was complaining of a headache, dizziness and nausea. She said her alcohol consumption the night before wasn't so much that she should be feeling this bad. It just didn't make sense, she insisted.

As Cunningham bagged Maria's pants for analysis later, she observed something resembling glue residue on the right buttock. She then examined the anus and genitalia. Both appeared normal. It was now necessary to take swabs from the vagina and cervix; a standard procedure, but one for which Cunningham, like most other doctors, had her own routine, her own groove.

She washed her hands and donned a fresh pair of gloves. On the metal trolley beside the bed she laid out the exact number of swabs and corresponding slides, which she labelled according to body parts. On this occasion she took four swab samples: two from the upper region of Maria's vagina, and another two from further up in her cervix. Afterwards she slotted each swab back in its plastic tubular sheath and laid them all out on the trolley.

Taking hold of the swabs again, she dabbed each onto its corresponding slide. These would be examined under the microscope for sperm, and the swabs analysed for DNA. She placed each cotton tip back into its sheath, snipping off the corners to let the air in. She took one last swab of the inside of Maria's cheek to provide a reference sample for police. Finally Cunningham placed the samples into specimen bags, sealed them with hospital stickers and signed the cover to tamper-proof the bundle. She handed the sealed bags to police, duly documenting the transaction. And with that, her task was done.

Porter placed the sealed bags, containing Maria's samples and Maria's pants in the property store at Doncaster police station. She locked the urine sample, collected from the Austin's pathology department, in the fridge.

The following Friday the sealed bags were deposited at the Victoria Police Forensic Services Department at Macleod in Melbourne's northeast. The urine sample went to the Institute of Forensic Medicine, where tests detected the presence of alcohol and two other drugs. One was the anti-nausea drug Maria was given at the hospital and the other, a prescription medication known commercially as Tegretol, which she began taking twelve years earlier for bipolar affective disorder, the condition known for many years as 'manic depression'. The tests came up negative for the most common date-rape drugs, but this was hardly definitive as far as the toxicologist was concerned, because the body tends to eliminate these substances so fast they rarely leave a trace.

In a witness statement, Maria would insist she had only been drunk three times in her life. One of those was when her nephew was diagnosed with a debilitating heart condition; Maria drowned her sorrows with the child's distraught mother. But she had never been this out of it, she swore, 'Never like this.'

'I don't *feel* like I've had sex,' Maria told police at the hospital. A few days later she noticed fresh bruises on her inner thighs, bruises that resembled *finger marks*.

She included the observation in a fresh police statement the following week and related her concerns to forensic physician Dr Janet Towns who, having been briefed by police that Maria was a suspected victim of drink spiking and sexual assault, photographed the bruises on the inner thighs, along with some others detected on the right shoulder blade.

The wrinkle in time for which Maria couldn't account—ten minutes, maybe, a half-hour at most—was now a black hole of self-doubt and thickening dread.

Chapter 5

The Victoria Police Forensic Services Centre in outer-suburban Macleod is a light-filled building of glass walls and neat partitions. Its architecture and design reflect the principles of transparency, enquiry and enlightenment; the values of science itself, in other words. In this building a staff of about three hundred examine more than 27,500 items of forensic evidence a year. According to the website, the centre is one of the largest providers of forensic services in the world.

And it was here around midday on the Friday after the nightclub incident that a police scientist wearing her regulation gown, gloves and mask, took the sealed bag containing Maria's samples out of the storage fridge. She walked along a series of corridors to the biological examination branch, arriving at a room of numbered benches, some with laminated tops and others of stainless steel. From its various vantage points, the room offers views of the ballistics branch, the tea room and an outdoor courtyard.

The scientist set the bag down on Bench 9 and removed the contents; all the samples Cunningham had taken when she examined Maria at the Austin hospital: Maria's cheek swab, the swabs from her vagina and cervix, and their four corresponding slides. She then took the slides to another bench, placing them on a rack under a sink, to treat each with a drop of purple solution. Once the solution had dried she washed it off, added a drop of a different solution, pink this time, and again waited for it to dry. This way she would be able to detect the presence of semen under the microscope: the sperm heads stain purple, the tails pink.

The scientist slipped the slides from Maria's vagina under the microscope and peered down the lens. Nothing suspicious there. She examined one of the cervical slides and again saw nothing unusual. Then, on the other slide from Maria's cervix she saw them: narrow slivers of purple. In her notes, following the usual procedure, she rated the number of sperm detected at 'medium'—more than zero, but less than four. She wrote, 'two-plus,' meaning 'a few' sperm and in accordance with protocol handed her findings to the case manager, forensic biologist Deborah Scott, who looked everything over and verified the conclusions as sound.

The following September, 2007, at the committal proceedings—the preliminary hearing about whether the Crown has a basic case against the accused—the magistrate asked Scott if she could 'put a number' on the amount of sperm found and preserved on the slide. Scott replied that, yes, she was willing to examine the slide again and determine precisely how many sperm were present, 'if it's relevant'. So, back at the lab, Scott peered down the microscope and counted on the slide about fifteen to seventeen sperm heads, and one sperm with tail intact. And once armed with these particulars she could confidently assert that, as sperm shed their tails after a day or so, intercourse in this instance had occurred *no more* than forty-eight hours before the medical examination, and most likely within the preceding twenty-four.

But the die had been cast on that first viewing. The case was now officially a rape investigation.

Chapter 6

After the negotiations with Jama fell apart, the transcript of his trial became my bible. I would eventually read it through like a novel, but initially turned to the evidence of Jama's alibi witnesses, especially his father, and to his uncle Osman's advocacy at the sentencing hearing.

The Jamas had been a well-connected family in Somalia. Their lives unravelled in 1991 when insurgent forces ousted the dictatorial regime of General Mohamed Siad Barre and the country finally plunged into outright civil war and anarchy; both Osman and Jama's father fell victim to violence and torture.

Such facts, however bleak, were at least concrete in nature. But another, more abstract exchange that took place during the sentencing hearing threw me. Osman was in the witness box, and Jama's barrister said to him: 'I want to ask you this. Being Somalian, has it been difficult in any way for Farah to live or integrate himself into the community?'

To which Osman replied: 'I believe Farah is a very nice boy who don't talk too much, he keeps always quiet and for the integration he integrates into the community …'

However many times I read these sentences—and I would ponder them from various angles—much of the meaning eluded me. The men seemed to be speaking thematically, acknowledging forces that were at work somewhere beyond the courtroom.

Was Jama 'integrated'? What did that buzz-word of the Howard years, promoted as a desirable alternative to 'multi-culturalism', really mean? And I wondered: was the barrister pleased with Osman's upbeat response or had he hoped he might say the opposite?

On Google Maps the Jama family home in Preston clicked into view. Solid red brick, untrimmed lawn in the front yard, classic suburbia. Only the multiple pairs of shoes—Jama is one of six children—outside the front door hinted at the culture of its inhabitants.

Apparently, the appearance of Somali families in the mid-1990s, one of the first large intake of refugees from the Horn of Africa, caused major headaches for Victoria's Office of Housing. The solid brick homes built in Heidelberg West for the 1956 Olympics were not designed for families of six to eight children. Hunched in front of my computer, staring hard at the Preston home with the runners and boots and sandals parked at the door, I recalled some friendly advice from a Somali man close to the Jamas. 'To understand what happened in this case, you have to try to walk in Somali shoes,' he had said. And yet the Somalis as a collective could hardly be more 'Other' in the Australian setting. Africans in a society unaccustomed to blacks; devout Sunni Muslims in a post 9/11 era; their cultural baggage weighed down by tribalism, polygamy, female circumcision, a savage civil war, a legacy of trauma. 'Because of the civil war,' Jama's counsel explained to the judge at sentencing, 'the family decided to move to Kenya as refugees.' I stopped reading. The barrister's use of the phrase 'decided to move' jarred. Do refugees 'decide' to move, or are they, by definition, forced to flee?

Consulting the map, it struck me that Somalia, the 637,657 square kilometres of land, hugging the Gulf of Eden all the way to the Indian Ocean on the East African coast, bounded by the Republic of Djibouti at its northeast, and Ethiopia and Kenya at its south and southwest, resembles a lopsided and gaping pair of scissor blades. News items from 'the world's most failed state' were almost always diabolical: a burgeoning piracy operation in the north-east, the al-Qaeda-affiliated Islamist insurgency of al-Shabab in the south; famine, brutality, human suffering on a massive scale. On the internet Somalia's recent history unfolds in a barrage of stats and images that create a nightmarish backdrop.

Somalia is a weeping wound, excelling only in the statistics of misery; a civil war that left an estimated half a million dead and about 1.7 million, roughly one-fifth of its population, displaced. More tragic still, the world did try to stem the bleeding on this occasion—too late, as always—but from 1992 to 1994, the US led a humanitarian intervention. Its ultimate failure was sufficiently spectacular for Hollywood's purposes.

I re-watched *Black Hawk Down*, which depicts the Battle

of Mogadishu, the ill-fated raid aimed at capturing warlord Mohamed Farrah Aidid. The gun-toting, gum-chewing, rocket-launching militiamen swarm plague-like from every dusty corner and rooftop; injured marines spill intestines over their comrades. After nearly two-and-a-half admittedly mesmerising hours, my temples pounded with nausea. At its release, *The New York Times*' critic said the film, shot in Morocco, 'reeks of glumly staged racism'.

The Jamas hail from Somalia's port capital, Mogadishu. Their clan affiliation was told to me as Darod Majerteen; a broad description, apparently, as this grouping branches to six sub-clans. It is shorthand typically provided to outsiders such as me, baffled by the very idea of tribal affiliation, at least in the genealogical sense. And typically for Somalis, the foundation story of the sub-clan purports to trace its lineage to an ancestor who fled unrest in Saudi Arabia and married a local Galla woman. Adam-and-Eve style mythology, an historian assured me. Legends linking Somalis to the bloodline of the Prophet Mohammed exist simply to say, 'We are good Muslims, we are not African'.

But the myths endure, seeping poison even here; Melbourne's Somali community riven with tribalism. A communal organisation for every sub-clan, that kind of thing. An insider's joke asserts that you can tell which clan a Somali belongs to from the first four digits of their phone number: the suburb says it all.

In another of those reports and journal papers that began

to crowd my desk, I came across a quote from an academic who had tried to elucidate the 'rules' and psychological demands of the clan system, with its ever-shifting alliances: 'I and my clan are against the world. I and my cousin are against the clan. I and my brother are against my cousin. I am against my brother'.

Jama was only four at the time of the family's flight in 1991 from Mogadishu to a refugee camp across the border in Kenya. In those years of deprivation and uncertainty, he was taught the Koran and given religious instruction, but received no formal schooling. By the time the mother, father and six children finally left the refugee camps for New Zealand seven years later, Jama was on the cusp of adolescence.

In New Zealand, they joined Osman, who had emigrated to the country three years before and now acted as their sponsor. At the sentencing hearing, Osman recounted that the family had been welcomed from the 'boat' at Wellington, though it's hard to tell in the transcript precisely what this meant, or even whether the words had been recorded accurately. He also recounted preparing his house for the Jamas' arrival. He said his brother and family ended up living with him for about two years, until he shifted across the Tasman to Australia and they once more followed in his footsteps. It was in New Zealand that Farah Jama, then aged eleven, had his first experience of primary school.

And so the Jamas arrived in Melbourne, settling first in Carlton and later in Preston, part of a wave of newcomers whose arrival, in a country that only a few decades earlier officially favoured white immigrants, created a dilemma for the Office of Housing.

Farah Jama attended high school at Peter Lalor Secondary College. He enjoyed playing cricket and basketball. At the sentencing hearing Osman told the judge that as a young adult Jama had aspired to join the army.

Something was said in my very first encounter with Osman, at the 2006 meeting with a handful of Somali community leaders. After a long discussion about the struggles and triumphs of Somali migrants in Melbourne, one of the other men, polite to the point of obsequious and quite formal in manner, asked, 'And where are *you* from?'

Would Australians of Anglo-Celtic stock consider the question an affront? For me, it's long been secret ethnics' business. We migrants, or children of migrants, smell of exile, not quite sure if we've just arrived or are just poised to leave. Our secret code is a restless melancholy, a longing for another, faraway place where we need never explain ourselves again and can finally be whole. It is a fantasy land, this forsaken 'homeland', a curse, really.

Perhaps I could stumble for some of the way in Somali shoes. I told the men, 'Hungarian', and while there were good reasons to leave it at that, I blurted, 'Hungarian, Jewish'.

The man gave a sugary smile.

'You know,' he said, almost conspiratorial, 'I will never forget that during the famine [in Somalia] Israel was the first country to send us aid, *the first country.*'

One afternoon, back in 2006, I had toured part of Jama's stomping ground in West Heidelberg—'toured', because for a southerner like me this pocket of Melbourne is akin to a foreign country. Actually, the cluster of shops known as The Mall was at one stage almost a little Somalia. I visited stores selling folk items: clogs, a wooden 'pillow' bracelet, talismans to ward off disease. On a pin board in a fast-food shop some wrinkled photos testified to an intimate heartache—a picture of Somali Airlines, another of the national soccer team—nostalgic souvenirs from the 1960s when the modern republic, newly born through the merger of former colonies British Somaliland and Italian Somaliland, could legitimately be referred to as a state. Now I wondered if Jama's teenage attraction to the army was partly the product of a displaced, subconscious fantasy of going back home and putting everything right.

Recently I was introduced to a slender and quietly elegant woman who spoke of her 'integration' as if it were an anniversary markable on a calendar. She told me she lived in Brighton, and I asked, as diplomatically as possible, how a Somali ended up living in the monied bayside suburb. 'The government gave me a house in Brighton,' she joked.

The Office of Housing accommodated her in neighbouring Hampton, her family virtually the only Africans in sight. Had she remained in the bosom of her community in Flemington she would never have integrated, she insisted. I understand the woman had become a sought-after public speaker, a hit on the Rotary circuit.

Had Farah Jama *integrated*? He was a 'hard worker', Osman pleaded before the judge. He had 'never been anti-social or anti-community'. Shunned alcohol, helped support his family. Played sport, studied, dreamed of joining the army. He finished school for crying out loud. Was this not enough? I wondered. What else would it take? Some Somali kids fail to graduate. They clash with police, chew khat, don't know where they belong. My friend Yusuf, who has a poetic sensibility, speaks of a generation 'lost to the street'. Jama was not one of those kids. He was well-behaved and popular. That's why, I heard over and over, what happened came as such a shock.

I called a man named Ibrahim Hussein who owns a warehouse in Preston. Farah Jama would often turn up during school holidays as part of his job for a removalist. The youth said he had to work because his father was debilitated.

'A very nice boy,' Hussein recalled, 'Very respectful … His family are very respectful people, his mother, his father … So really when I saw him on the news with all this business I was shocked.'

As I thanked Hussein for his time and tried to wind up the conversation, he asked if I would perhaps be interested in writing the story of a friend of his next.

'He's a refugee from Somalia,' Hussein explained. 'You know how he got here? He hid on a ship! You know where? You know the big fan in the top of the ship, the pipe, the duct that the smoke comes out of? He was like that! No food! No water! Nothing! From Mogadishu! He didn't even know where the ship was going!'

I asked Hussein what the man was up to in Melbourne. Did he work?

'No,' Hussein said. 'He doesn't work now, he's too depressed. He's very depressed, very traumatised … So Julie, maybe after you finish the book you can write this story next, yes?'

Yes, I said, maybe I'd write that story next.

※

Jama's counsel asked Osman in court: 'Are the matters that I've put about his [Jama's] background, his development, the places where he lived et cetera, is all that correct?'

Osman stammered, his usually solid English straining under the earnestness.

'They are all correct and I will add that he has never, ever, even sentencing from this court. He has never done a trouble in school, even one day during his primary school and secondary school. You can ask his headmaster or teachers for the—'

The barrister cut him off.

Chapter 7

Many people would be familiar with the image of a DNA molecule—two strands wrapped around one another, the double helix. Curled up, these strands form the nucleus of a human cell. The caption on such pictures usually reads 'the blueprint for life' or something similar that invites us to marvel at the scientific quest to crack the human genetic code.

The DNA strands are inherited, one set from the father and another from the mother. Some parts of the DNA strands are genes, which code for proteins, the little machines that build our cells and determine whether we have blue eyes or black hair or a propensity to be musical. The remainder of the strands don't seem to code for anything, but have scattered within them clusters of repeats. The number of repeats varies widely between individuals, and it's this variation that interests criminal investigators. Victorian scientists measure the number of repeats at nine sites along the two strands. From this they derive an individual's DNA 'profile', reported as nine pairs of numbers, eighteen in total.

For present purposes, all we need to understand is that

this eighteen-number profile is different for almost every person and can be easily compared to others on a police database.

Once Maria's slides were inspected under the microscope for sperm, her swabs underwent DNA testing in the biological examination branch of the police laboratory. This is an area notable for the rule that samples must progress through the space in only one direction. Backtracking is strictly forbidden. So, Maria's swabs came out of storage, their cotton heads were snapped off and placed into tubes, the swabs from her vagina in one, those from her cervix in another. They were treated with an enzyme and a chemical to extract the DNA and separate any sperm cells from other human cells.

The results of the DNA tests would prove the swabs from Maria's cervix indeed yielded sperm. The swabs from her vagina did not. Seen in isolation, the discrepancy is neither unusual nor curious. The vagina is an acidic and hostile environment for sperm, the cervix is less so. Sperm that reach the neck of the womb can survive there for considerably longer periods. As far as the forensic experts were concerned, nothing seemed amiss.

The DNA was quantified and amplified, a section of the chromosomal strand magnified and replicated, again and again, in a process analogous to photocopying. An electrophoresis machine ran currents through the DNA to separate the fragments, which could now be measured to identify the patterns of repeats at the critical nine sites along the strand.

The end result of this process is a graph of peaks and troughs that vaguely resembles an electrocardiogram. The co-ordinates, the sets of seemingly random numbers, at least to the untrained eye, constitute a profile that distinguishes one human being on the planet from another. Or in this instance, an individual with DNA patterns 18 and 19, and 22 and 27, and so on across the nine sites.

The marks of a wanted man.

※

In the popular cop-show franchise CSI, complicated forensic procedures are completed at the speed of light as the action zips from the discovery of a crime to the handcuffed culprit within the space of fifty minutes. It is trite to say lead times are considerably longer in real world laboratories, but it still surprised me to learn that with sex offences, the period between police forensics taking receipt of a sample to their obtaining a DNA profile of a suspect is typically six weeks. In this respect, Maria's was a typical case.

On 8 September 2006 scientists at the forensics lab convened, as they do most mornings, for the procedure known as a 'match run'. They entered the latest batch of DNA profiles, each unique, eighteen-number sequence, onto the police database. The new profiles would be automatically compared to the tens of thousands of profiles of other known suspects and offenders. Included in the fresh batch that morning was the DNA profile the scientists had obtained from the sperm found on Maria's cervical swabs.

The following morning, in accordance with standard

procedure, the scientists examined the database again for the results of the previous day's match run. They saw a spreadsheet report that attested to an unambiguous result. The profile obtained from Maria's swabs came up a perfect match to another profile that had been placed on the police database the previous month as a result of a totally unrelated criminal investigation that went nowhere.

It identified a Somali teenager, Farah Jama.

Deborah Scott, the forensic biologist, took charge of the final steps in the scientific process. She double-checked the results of the DNA profiling and, finding everything in order, signed off on them. As is also routine, she fed the information into the computer to obtain relative probabilities for two different propositions: one, that the sample from the crime scene, in this instance Maria's cervix, came from Farah Jama, and two, that the sample from the crime scene came from an unknown Caucasian male in Australia who, by coincidence, just happened to share Jama's profile.

About a year later at the request of Detective Karen Porter, and also for the sake of 'rigour', as Scott would put it in court, she repeated the analysis only this time she substituted the unknown Caucasian male with an unknown Somali. To brutally paraphrase the results: the likelihood that the crime scene sample came from Farah Jama was beyond overwhelming, whereas the likelihood that it came from another man, whether of Somali ethnicity or any other, who just happened to share Jama's profile, was spectacularly remote.

Chapter 8

At 7.50 am one November morning, four months after Maria was found unconscious in the toilet cubicle, Detective Karen Porter and two of her male colleagues, fronted the Jama family home in Raglan Street, Preston. The detectives asked to speak with Farah Jama. The young man came to the door. His parents and sisters gathered round, listening.

'Are you Farah?' Porter asked.

'Yes.'

Porter introduced herself. She said an allegation had been made about the rape of a woman at Hotel Shoppingtown at Doncaster.

'I need to speak to you about it,' Porter said. 'Have you ever been to the Venue 28 nightclub at Hotel Shoppingtown in Doncaster?'

'No,' Jama replied.

'Well, have you ever been to the Doncaster area?'

'No.'

Porter told Jama that he was under arrest and would be

taken to Doncaster police station for a formal interview. She informed him of his rights and gave him a caution. Perhaps he would like to phone someone first? The youth said no, he would not. The four of them piled into an unmarked police car, with Jama told to sit in the back. Jama's mother and one of his sisters followed close behind in their own car.

Porter asked Jama if his English was good.

'Pretty good,' he said.

Would he like an interpreter for the interview?

'What's that?' Jama asked.

'Someone to help you with your English.'

No, he didn't want an interpreter.

They drove towards Doncaster, a suburb fifteen kilometres away, an area of Rococo mansions and migrants made good. En route, they approached Doncaster Shopping Centre. Porter drew Jama's attention to it.

'It's there on the left,' she said. 'Have you ever been there before?'

'No.' Jama replied.

They took a detour down the driveway and through the car park of Hotel Shoppingtown to level two, the entrance to Venue 28.

Again Porter tried: 'Farah, this is the entrance to the nightclub where the rape took place. Have you ever been there?'

'Never.'

At Doncaster station, the police ushered Jama into an interview room. His mother and sister waited outside at reception. Porter asked Jama where he was on Saturday, 15

July, the night of the drama in Doncaster. Jama wasn't sure. So she tried to jog his memory, to orient him in time.

'Now, I'll help you a little bit with that. I know where you were on 14 July. Do you remember that you went out with a couple of friends? I'm going to be really bad with these names, but Abdulkadir Abdullah?'

'Yeah.'

'And Abdulkadir Mohamed?'

'Yeah.'

Porter was talking about the night Jama, and the two friends she had named, had hooked up with a young woman they met in a pool hall in Reservoir. The young woman went to the police that same night and alleged she had been forced to perform oral sex. Questioned the following week, Jama admitted to sexual contact, but insisted it was consensual. Jama's friends each separately backed his account. When police again questioned the woman she largely conceded the boys' version of events and withdrew her complaint. The matter ended there, but it was during this investigation that police first obtained samples of Jama's DNA.

For Porter, the significance of the sexual assault complaint was that it had occurred on Friday 14 July, the *night before* the Doncaster incident. At this stage, though, the chronology was only significant for her as a prompt and a grounding device, as a logical place from which to start her interrogation. Once the interview concluded, Porter sought Jama's consent to supply police with yet another DNA sample. He obediently scraped the inside of his cheek with a swab.

Three days later Porter lodged the sample at the police

forensics lab in Macleod. It awaited analysis but the ritual was mere formality, the end result hardly in doubt. Jama's DNA profile already matched the sample recovered from Maria's cervix, and DNA does not lie. Still, the case was troubling Porter.

After Jama's interview, she ran checks on his car, a white, 1989 Honda Prelude coupe, for any parking tickets or speeding fines around the Doncaster area on 15 July. The search came up blank. She requested from Optus a log of calls made from his pre-paid mobile account on the night, along with the cell tower locations to see if the calls were made around Doncaster. Nothing again, though, as she would tell the Magistrate at Jama's committal, she could not obtain information about where calls might have been received on the night because it would have cost $200, 'and there have to be extenuating circumstances for that to be authorised by the department.' Nor could she search bank accounts for possible withdrawals in the Doncaster area because as Jama had told them, he didn't own a bank account.

The truth was that Porter had been unable to find any corroborating evidence to link Jama to the club. She had dusted the venue for fingerprints, especially the toilets, scoured both sides of the cubicle partition where Maria had been found, and done the same for the adjoining one. She checked the top surface of the partition where you would expect someone climbing over to take hold with their hands. All she found were some dainty prints presumed to be those of Stephanie Johnstone, the nightclub supervisor.

Then there was the security footage from the club entrance,

the only door through which the public could get in or out of the place. On viewing it she noticed there were time gaps. She returned to the nightclub and asked the staff to find more footage from the night. She noted Maria arriving at the club, together with Sophie and Alex; the victim stood out in her long coat with fur at the collar and cuffs, her relatively large frame and long, straight hair. Porter froze the image and created a still. She didn't see Maria's exit from the premises on the film, but apparently she had been carried to the ambulance via a back-stage door, so that made sense. The rest of the footage she watched in real time, frame by frame, over and over, for any sign of a black teenager. Nothing.

Later Porter discovered the footage was still incomplete. It started from 9.30 pm even though the club opened at eight. A half-hour period from 11 pm to 11.30 pm was also missing, with no film past 11.45 pm, even though the venue did not close its doors until 4 am. But by then more than a month had elapsed, and the venue was no longer obliged to retain the footage.

The cameras inside the venue revealed nothing either, just the occasional flash of a strobe light and people milling around. It was of zero evidentiary value, but, as Porter wryly remarked at the committal, the cameras looked good on the club's licence. And Maria had clearly never seen the young guy before. At Porter's request, she attended Doncaster station in mid-October to look at a photoboard of African men. Jama's face was among them. Maria shook her head. No, she couldn't identify any of them.

'And I didn't speak to any black men,' she added.

Porter spoke to a security guard from the club, but he remembered nothing about the incident. Another guard, a bloke by the name of Tommy, couldn't recognise any of the faces either.

In April the following year, Porter went one step further and contacted the other two Somali men who had also been on the scene of the pool hall incident the night before the events in Doncaster. She swung past the house of one the men, Abdulkadir Mohamed and left her card. He waited till twenty past eleven one night to ring her back. Both men claimed they had never accompanied Jama to Doncaster, let alone to the nightclub at Hotel Shoppingtown. They had never even been to Doncaster on their own. And in an exchange that would prove significant at Jama's trial, Porter also asked Mohamed if he recalled going anywhere on Saturday, July 15, the night after the pool hall episode. No, Mohamed said. He didn't go anywhere that night.

Porter pursued one last avenue of inquiry. She assumed the DNA samples from the pool hall incident, samples that contained Jama's DNA, would have been processed in the police lab at around the same time as Maria's. She couldn't ignore this apparent coincidence. Especially given the atmosphere of nervous vigilance around forensics.

The previous month the Coroner delivered his findings from the inquest into the death of the Victorian toddler Jaidyn Leskie. One issue in the inquest was the police lab's discovery on the toddler's clothing of DNA matching that of a rape victim in a totally unrelated case. Although the samples from the two cases were examined by the same scientist within a close time frame, the lab had steadfastly rejected contamination as a possibility. Police forensics instead argued the DNA pointed to a mystery woman, somehow connected with the toddler's death, who coincidentally had the same or similar DNA as the rape victim. The police stuck with the theory, notwithstanding that the chances of such an 'adventitious match' occurring were, according to one independent expert, as small as one in 3.4 billion.

The Coroner found that the DNA match was indeed the result of contamination which 'had clearly occurred somewhere in the laboratory process', and dismissed the alternative explanation as a possibility 'so slender as to be practically meaningless'. Moreover, he pronounced the lab's extreme defensiveness in response to the mere suggestion of a flaw in its processes a matter of 'potential concern for the criminal justice system'. The high-profile foul-up subjected the lab to intense scrutiny, its processes and track record thrust under the microscope.

So against this background, Porter, clearly a prudent sort, first raised Jama's case with her superior, Detective Senior Sergeant Neil Beeson, and then wrote what is colloquially referred to as a 'cover-your-arse' memo. Setting out the circumstances of the two separate, but proximate, investigations, she asked whether Maria's sample may have been contaminated at the police lab. Beeson passed on Porter's memo, along with a covering memo of his own, to the manager of the lab's Biological Examination Branch. An alleged offender had been identified through a DNA sample, Beeson wrote by way of summary, but the alleged offender was denying he even knew the victim, while for her part the victim had no or little recollection of the night:

> In the current climate I need to be able to discount the possibility of cross-contamination. Perhaps a report is all that is required. I have every faith in the process but no doubt the subject will be raised at any subsequent trial so we may as well be armed with suitable answers to the inevitable questions.

The response came directly from the case manager, Deborah Scott:

> In my opinion, I do not think contamination between the two cases could have occurred. Items from the two cases and the relevant reference samples [Jama's cheek swabs] were examined at different times, at different areas and by different people. Also the DNA processes were done at different times such that the samples were not processed together in the same batch. If you need a report and any clarification, please do not hesitate to contact me.

Scott's response was somewhat less than thorough. She did not offer a chronology, which would have confirmed that the samples were received in the lab and tested within days of each other. She did not reveal the two samples had a common case manager—herself, in fact!—who had signed both in, and signed off on both sets of tests. She did not disclose the scope of her internal review or hedge or caveat her response in any way. Despite the 'climate of the times' her response heeded nothing of the Coroner's warning about the lab's problematic internal culture. She gave an admittedly narrow question a narrow response.

Her assurances, accepted without further requests for clarification, undoubtedly influenced all that came later even though they shouldn't have. For whatever the shortcomings of Scott's reply, her share of the responsibility for Jama's fate ought to be regarded as slight. After all, the case manager was right: the sample from the pool hall woman was tested, four days after her complaint, on Bench 1 of the lab, while Maria's samples appeared two days later on Bench 9; a good twenty-five metres, walls and other infrastructure, separated the two work stations. The possibility of contamination between the two was negligible.

Once more dotting the i's and crossing the t's, Porter prepared a brief of evidence pointing out that a criminal prosecution against Jama would be heavily, if not entirely, dependent on DNA evidence. The brief was approved and sent to the Office of Public Prosecutions, which has a specialist unit that handles sex offences. Cases that arrive here are assessed for their complexity and farmed out to individual solicitors.

The case was certainly deemed noteworthy. Never before had prosecutors gone after an offender solely on the basis of DNA evidence, in the absence of any corroborating evidence. An investigation of the file years later, once the Jama scandal had come to light, turned up a memo written by a lawyer in the OPP: 'Case appears to be 100% DNA evidence; should at least run it past [senior barrister] Michelle Williams SC'. The senior barrister was not consulted, however. Instead, prosecutors asked more questions about procedures in the police lab, and again the results appeared unimpeachable.

But the prosecution was more worried about something else. These worries were also expressed in a memo, this time to the prosecutor in charge of the committal. According to the laws of evidence, any irrelevant or prejudicial material, which might reflect badly on the accused, had to be kept out of the proceedings. So, the memo read, the prosecution faced the 'difficulty' of how to present the DNA evidence against Jama without disclosing why the police held his sample at all.

The prosecutor would have to skillfully avoid any mention of the pool hall incident in the courtroom.

Chapter 9

While a rough portrait of the Jama family was emerging from my research, I thirsted to know more about their flight from civil war, their journey out of Africa. How had they managed to cross the border to Kenya? Perhaps they travelled by boat some of the way, perhaps they crossed the entire 531 kilometres, roughly the distance from Coffs Harbour to Noosa Heads, on land.

After Siad Barre's fall, hundreds of thousands of Somalis made the treacherous overland journey on foot. Some mothers were forced to choose between their children. Some children had to be left behind. I once asked a Somali woman, who in the course of our conversation abruptly lifted her layers of garments to show me thighs dimpled with bullet holes, how many children she had. 'Eight alive,' was her answer.

The flight from Somalia is a fraught subject. We outsiders are cautioned to approach delicately; let them skate over it if necessary. As a woman, however, I have some latitude; I can ask a Somali woman how many children she has. The less fragile among them might say something such as 'eight alive'. In other instances, I may have to wait a while and then, in another context, gently ask, 'And how many children live with you now?'

The men, wracked with guilt, convinced they failed as providers, may refuse to talk about it at all. This was but one of the cautionary guidelines imparted to me. Somalis of a certain generation struggle with free and frank conversation. Wives may keep silent before husbands, children before parents. Some things are never spoken of.

The point during Jama's sentencing hearing when Osman, giving evidence as the youth's uncle, told of the leadership positions he held in the refugee camps, evokes a strange sense of pathos. I read over the passage in the transcript a number of times partly for this reason, and partly to gather leads.

Osman was asked by Jama's counsel to confirm he had been 'closely associated' with the boy and his family. He was then asked why the Jamas went to New Zealand before they eventually settled in Australia.

'Because I start willfully from our country on 1991 together because we were two brothers, family, and we went to Kenya. I was head of one section in Leboyer camp. We then lived at another camp, which in Mombasa, called Otanga refugee camp and I was the vice chairperson in that camp for four years.'

After a time I figured 'Leboyer', spelt phonetically in the transcript, was a reference to the transit camp of Liboi, a dusty town about eighteen kilometres from the Somali border, through which at least 200,000 Somalis passed during the early years of the civil war.

And 'Otanga' was almost certainly 'Utange', a camp on the outskirts of the city of Mombasa. I was told the Jama family spent several years there, alongside other refugees of the Darod clan, most having fled from Mogadishu or Kismayu to escape revenge killings by rival clans. They were mostly urban and middle-class, merchants or former army officers; cashed-up and well-connected overseas. Many were reasonably optimistic about their prospects and believed their stay in the camp would be short. The atmosphere in Utange in those early months was not one of complete despair.

Presumably, after seven years in the camps, the Jamas' mood soured; their faith in the efficiency and benevolence of UN agencies and Western governments tested. Could I presume at least this much? I made some effort to find out about Utange. I chased The International Federation of Red Cross and Red Crescent Societies and the United Nations High Commissioner for Refugees, hoping they might track down an aid worker who remembered what life was like in the camp. My email query bounced between bureaucracies in Sydney, Geneva, Nairobi. But it was too long ago, everyone said. People in this line of work burn out fast. Perhaps if I rang so-and-so from the BBC … well, he might know of someone who knows of someone …

In the end, I did not call the journalist from the BBC. It seemed all too hard, and unlikely to yield any great insight. After all, if I called the journalist would it earn me the right to extrapolate platitudes about the Jama family such as: 'After seven years in refugee camps, they dreamed of a better life'. Or: 'Seven years in refugee camps left the family traumatised and fearful and made it hard for them to *integrate* into a new society …'

In her book, *Up We Grew: Stories of Australian Childhoods*, my late colleague Pamela Bone interviews a man whose family, upon fleeing Somalia, also passed through Utange. He recalls thousands upon thousands of people 'sleeping just on the ground under the trees … no water, no sanitation.' The UN would bring corn and rice, but sometimes food was scarce. Near the camp were wild animals: hyenas, lions, wild dogs. They could be heard howling at night. Sometimes the animals killed people. After burial, the wild dogs would dig up the bodies.

I stumbled on a UNHCR briefing paper on Utange. Entitled 'Site Profile', it dated from two years after the outbreak of civil war. 'The number of registered refugees at Utange are 18,581,' the paper began. 'In addition there are some 8200 unregistered refugees who are being gradually transferred to Marafa.' The document was a battery of facts conveyed in a detached, staccato manner. Utange occupied fifteen acres of land; ninety per cent of its population was Muslim, most of the water was piped from a treatment works 120 kilometres from Mombasa, some 5000 cubic metres of piped water were consumed in the camp each month. In the same, clinical tone came a hint of perpetual crisis: 'During frequent breakdowns on the main pipeline three water tankers have been used for trucking of water to the camp'.

Through the steady accumulation of detail, the camp, as if by an act of defiance, began to spring to life, to teem with humanity. Shelters in a style common to the coastal region were erected from Makuti (palm leaves), sticks and mud. A large camp clinic, with a local refugee staff of about a dozen Somali doctors and several nurses, treated about three hundred patients a day. There was also a tuberculosis and maternal and child health unit, a supplementary feeding centre and an observation ward for a handful of in-patients. A 'well organised' refugee primary school catered for all the grades.

According to Osman, Jama had 'no formal schooling' in the camp. My sketchy timeline suggested Jama may still have been too young to start school in Utange. When four years later the camp, besieged with fighting between rival Somali groups, was closed by the Kenyan government, Osman had already left for New Zealand. Where the Jamas spent their last two years or so in Kenya, I couldn't tell.

The section headed 'Sanitation' caught my attention:
> Garbage collection is done four times a day to minimise the risk of any epidemic outbreak. The careless attitude of refugees towards the disposal of waster [sic] water is of serious concern and the presence of heaps of soil for mudding has worsened the situation. Therefore it has been decided that

Murram [a form of clayey material used for road surfaces in tropical Africa] be spread in all areas that cause a hazardous situation.

The words 'careless attitude' injected emotion into an otherwise sterile accounting, the writer suddenly chiding and schoolmarmish, as if their exasperation and weariness had finally reached bursting point. More than anything it was these words that hammered home the loss of dignity, the overwhelming sense of helplessness, which is the lot of the stateless and destitute.

'There were common toilets,' said Yasin Farah, a Melbourne resident who was also a refugee in Utange during those years. I had called him up to ask what life was like there; we spoke for a few minutes.

'Very mess you know. Insects, infections … mud … the larvae goes on your feet. You know what I am talking about yes? Err … I think if you never been in a such a place, you can't know.'

He hesitated.

'I remember there was a fire always there in Utange because people were cooking in their homes and it was always windy and a lot of homes were burnt and many people became homeless … and there no fire brigade came.'

For some decades, before Somalia's civil war and refugee crisis, Australia's Somali population amounted to one man,

Abdullahi Ayan. These days he is revered as the 'father' of Somalis in Australia. I met the once lonely pioneer at a function shortly after I had met Jama himself. Ayan, who arrived in Western Australia as a high school student in 1970, is short, partly bald and thin-boned. He speaks with a bouncy, confident energy. On this night he wore an aqua jumper and glasses as round as his face and was accompanied by his Anglo-Australian wife. I assumed he ranked among the *integrated*.

The function was a graduation ceremony for Somali students held at Victoria's Parliament House. My friend Yusuf had organised the event, the second of its kind, and had kindly asked me along.

'Contrary to rumours among the Somali community, I am not the first Somali in Australia,' Ayan told the assembly, 'even though for most of the 1970s I may have been the only one in Australia. A man from a well-known family from Northern Somalia had lived and worked in Australia as a shearer from around 1905 to 1906. He had been a stowaway on a ship he thought was taking him to Britain, but landed instead in Perth.'

Ayan spoke of racism and exclusion and the attack on multiculturalism. About the challenges facing young people. About older Somalis whose dreams of one day returning home were 'receding further and further into the horizon'. He diagnosed his community as suffering 'from deep-seated psychological problems—a collective psychosis'. They grieve the loss of their state, while denying their own complicity in its demise. Even here, he noted, the community perpetuates the clan divisions.

His words echoed in Queen's Hall as the graduates stepped forward one at a time to shake the hands of elders and political dignitaries. They posed for photos, cheeks flushed, faces beaming, parents and relatives looking on adoringly. These were kids who grew up in refugee camps, who perhaps once struggled to hold a pen or tell the time, or who nominated their birthday as January 1 because no one really knew. They were equal in prestige; teenagers who, like Jama, aspired to a TAFE course or had already attained a diploma from a technical college, were honoured alongside graduates of medicine.

An egalitarian spirit, born of shared deprivation, was on display.

'We came from Somalia,' one university student in a pink headscarf told the assembled, her voice euphoric. 'We shared classrooms with kids from Australia, we were assessed the same as them … and here we are!'

Through all this I sat among the women—the hall having been split between the genders—near the portrait of the affable former premier, Steve Bracks, and struggled to contain some powerful emotions. I was moved, of course, by the swell of pride in the room, but shame also curdled inside me. I was remembering my own university graduation. The weather gods had smiled on us, sunshine dappled through the branches of Melbourne University's English elms and danced over its Neo-Gothic turrets. My mother, herself once a refugee who had arrived here and worked ferociously and triumphed by graduating in medicine from the same hallowed institution, said, 'I'll always remember this day'. Meaning the day of my graduation. Her eyes were moist. I, on the other hand, felt compelled to affect insouciance, giving a 'whatever' shrug, as if the occasion was simply to be endured. It was the ugly ambivalence of the privileged.

Kath Kenny, assistant principal at Peter Lalor Secondary College, Jama's alma mater in Melbourne's north, kindly agreed to a meeting in the last week of Term One. It was a busy time, although when I arrived the school day was done and the place quiet. Two students, both boys, waited outside her office to settle some brief business. I strolled up and down the hallway for a few minutes, peeking into deserted classrooms, the chairs stacked on desks. On a pinboard, I noted a certificate for student finalists in a short film competition. An anti-racism poster on a wall featured a pair of smiling girls in hijab.

Even emptied of students, the place had a friendly, unimposing vibe. The brown concrete and brick building, single-storey and with a low roof, had a lived-in feel. A spanking new trade training centre was planned for the coming year. Peter Lalor had returned to its roots as a tech school, its first incarnation from 1968 to 1990, after declining enrolments and its last great hope, a merger with another local high school, fell through at the eleventh hour. Apparently the Lalor locals were happy with the outcome. Having attended the old tech school themselves, they liked the idea of their kids doing the same.

Kenny, middle-aged, her short hair streaked with grey, came to greet me. Dressed in pants and windcheater, she struck me instantly as honest and unaffected. Perhaps a little weary, as is often the case. The tougher the school, the more tired the school official.

'I'm not sure how much I can help you,' she said, as we settled at the round conference table in her office. 'I didn't have very much to do with Farah. I remember hearing suggestions he had been arrested. I think I probably heard about it at the end-of-year valedictory dinner and wondered if it was true. From time to time things like that happen. It might come to our attention later when people are looking for character references or we're told to make sure a student attends school because their case is coming up. So there was an awareness of something going on, but it wasn't hugely unusual … But later when I heard he was gaoled, I was shocked.'

Jama tended to keep a low profile, Kenny remembered. He was one of a bunch of boys who saw their future in a trade or vocation, rather than in academia.

'You just keep your eye out for them. Make sure they're in class when they should be.'

In the end, he did 'surprisingly well' given his background. He passed most of his regular subjects in Year 11 and switched to tech-oriented study the following year.

I told her about Jama's mysterious quip about how he could tell me tales from school that would 'blow my mind'.

She grinned. 'It would probably blow my mind too.'

She tried to recall any contemporaneous scandals. Occasional trouble at Thomastown and Epping train stations.

Some wayward kids hanging around Epping Plaza. One day she received a tip-off about an imminent showdown at Lalor station—one kid would be 'getting' another that very afternoon.

'So I drove down there in my car, but … nothing. Either the boys could see me coming or there was some other reason.' She smiled again.

Kenny pulled out a photo board from Jama's final year at Peter Lalor that featured a shot of every student in the school. She mentioned some recent statistics that showed the Peter Lalor catchment was 'the lowest socio-eco pocket' in the municipality of Whittlesea. I didn't need to ask what that meant—more single-parent or jobless families, more welfare recipients, more migrants of non-English speaking backgrounds. We bent over the photograph, scanned the names and faces. A sprinkling of 'skips', the odd 'Anderson' and 'Andrews', but otherwise a mosaic of shades and ethnicities. How many of them would be considered 'integrated'?

On the board next to Jama was a photo of a Zeinab Jama, an attractive girl with almond-shaped eyes, her face framed in a pink headscarf: Farah's sister, who, I learned later, married soon after leaving school. As for Jama, he is typically defiant, unsmiling, head tilted up and slightly back, eyebrows raised. I couldn't suppress the thought that this was probably what he had looked like in his mugshot.

Kenny sighed, 'I would hate to think he is cowed by his experience.'

'Oh, don't worry,' I assured her. 'He isn't cowed.'

Chapter 10

As the wheels of the criminal justice system tend to turn slowly, it took until May 2007, a full six months after Jama's arrest, before he was charged with rape. Four months later his case went to a closed committal hearing in Melbourne's Magistrates' Court, at which a barrister called Ian Crisp appeared for Jama, the defendant.

Barristers have considerable latitude at committals; the answers to their questions carry fewer consequences than at trial and the parties are freer to chase little-known or incomplete strands of evidence. And the proceedings at Jama's committal left me feeling that minds were possibly still open enough for serious doubt to intrude and dismantle the chimera of evidence assembled against him. Yet in the brisk informality of the Magistrates' Court, Jama's last real chance slipped away.

The Magistrate, Julian Francis Fitz-Gerald, advised Maria of her right under law to give evidence via a remote TV camera. Did she nevertheless wish to give evidence in open court? Maria said she did. Then perhaps she might prefer a screen be placed between her and the man charged with her rape? No, Maria insisted. She wished to face her alleged attacker. It was a show of guts under the circumstances. Given some of the questions lobbed at her on this day, the experience must have been gruelling.

During her cross-examination by Crisp she was handed a floor plan of Venue 28 and some photographs of the standing tables near the various bars. She was asked to identify the table at which she remembered talking to the two men, including the 'sleazy' one: her last memory before blacking out.

'I do not think it was *this* table,' said Maria, in the idiosyncratic phraseology I eventually recognised as hers. 'Because this seems to be, according to a diagram, in proximity to Bar Three and I maintain I was near Bar Two.' Maria marked on the diagram the table near Bar Two where she believed she had stood with the men. She marked the female toilets, 'some distance away from Bar Two', in which she had been found unconscious.

Next came Stephanie Johnstone, the nightclub supervisor. She affirmed her police statement while adding that it 'was a long time ago so my memory is a little bit vague on the whole thing'. Jama's counsel asked her about the number of patrons at the club that night.

'Just before 10.50 pm, would it be correct to say that there would've been a large number of people between the area of Bar Two and the female toilet that you've pointed out?'

Johnstone agreed that would be correct.

'In the hundreds of people, perhaps?'

'Yes.'

'So that for a person to get from that area of Bar Two across to the female toilet just before 10.50, they would have to find their way through a large number of people?'

'Yes.'

She confirmed there was only one public entrance to the venue. She answered questions about where she and the guards had gripped Maria's body when they slid her off the cubicle door and carried her to the backstage area. The prosecutor, asked, 'Did anyone at any stage have hold of her around her inner thighs?'

'Not that I know of, no,' Johnstone said.

'Near her crotch?'

'No.'

Police forensic biologist Deborah Scott appeared in the box. Now Crisp, Jama's counsel, angled and prodded and attacked and retreated. He lost the scent, ambled about and circled again. He verged on the killer questions. So semen was only detected on one of the microscope slides. Correct? Correct, Scott confirmed.

So unless he's mistaken, four swabs were taken from Maria and only a few sperm heads were found on just one swab? No, not on the swab, Scott explained, just on the slide. The swabs were submitted for DNA analysis, the swabs weren't checked for semen, only the slides were checked under the microscope for semen. And yes, only one of the slides showed up positive for semen.

Crisp also asked Nicola Cunningham, the forensic medical officer who examined Maria at the Austin, whether she had detected 'any spermatozoa within this subject?' Cunningham said no, she had not, though it was near impossible to see sperm with the naked eye.

Years later, after everything came to light, Crisp surely kicked himself for not stripping such questions, the ones he asked of both Cunningham and Scott, down to starting propositions and missing the wood for the trees. Perhaps he should have asked whether the scientist or the doctor thought it odd that sperm was found on only one of the four slides. Or, more specifically, whether they thought it odd that sperm showed up on just one of two slides made of swabs taken from Maria's cervix. Both swabs were of the same body region, so why did the results differ?

Perhaps he should have asked the scientist about the amount of sperm found on the slide. Admittedly, Scott's evidence on this score was difficult to comprehend as she was yet to properly count the sperm and could speak only of 'two-plus' sperm heads, a quantity she described as 'medium'. Nevertheless, perhaps Crisp still should have asked whether it struck her as odd that such a small amount was found when a normal ejaculation contains millions of sperm.

Perhaps he should have asked a host of painfully simple questions. But in truth the Prosecution had already managed to impress upon him some tragically flawed assumptions.

Cunningham agreed to assist the court in interpreting the results of Maria's urine screen, although this was not strictly speaking her area of expertise. She confirmed one of the drugs tested for was 'Gamma-hydroxybutyrate, more commonly known by people as GBH or GHB … known as a date-rape drug'.

The Magistrate seized the opportunity to share some uncertain thoughts with Cunningham.

'Doctor, you don't necessarily have to answer this but it's an interesting situation.' A witness has a couple of Frangelicos in a car, the Magistrate explained, another couple in a club, sometime between ten and eleven at night, and then blacks out. And then a urine sample is taken, and the only substance it turns up is alcohol. And, yes, he understands that's not necessarily surprising because the urine sample was taken about eight or so hours after the incident and date rape drugs tend to be flushed from the body quickly.

'It's a bit intriguing, though. Although perhaps it's just not intriguing and it's not surprising …'

It is the Magistrate's choice of adjectives that stands out most: was this case interesting or intriguing or surprising, or was it none of those things?

Of all the witnesses cross-examined at the committal, Porter's evidence was perhaps the most illuminating. Crisp touched on where and how the alleged rape was committed. Did Porter agree the rapist could only have left the cubicle by climbing over the wall? Well, yes, but she didn't think Maria was actually raped in the cubicle. Nor did she think it likely that someone had steered Maria to the toilets. There was simply no evidence that showed 'conclusively' where a sexual assault might have occurred.

As Crisp continued to cross-examine Porter, he stumbled on a fact he deemed significant. On the fateful night, Maria wasn't wearing any underwear.

'Are you suggesting she didn't have any underwear, at all? Only the trousers and that's all?'

'Yes, that's right,' said Porter.

Well, did Porter question her about why she didn't wear underpants? No, Porter did not. Did the detective view this as unusual? Not at all, Porter retorted. Some women simply don't want their underwear visible when they're wearing tight trousers.

Crisp pressed the detective, 'But some women wear G-strings?'

Crisp's questioning left me flummoxed. To be fair, it is his job to fish for anything that might cast doubt on the case against the accused, to muddy the waters. Still, it was hard to read him. Was he for real in describing Maria's lack of underwear, beneath *pants*, as 'unusual'? Was his shock at Maria having shunned *even a G-string*, authentic? But if Crisp knew all about G-strings then why was he so stunned that a woman had gone one step further, to bare comfort?

Either way, the effect was theatrical. Crisp hardly needed to spell it out, I thought. The suggestion hung in the air. *She wanted it.*

Nonetheless, the theatrics ultimately amounted to zero. Farah Jama was duly committed to stand trial.

Chapter 11

Between the day of Jama's arrest and his trial, a period of precisely eighteen months, the teenager struggled to come to terms with the surreal catastrophe that had derailed his life. Stress threatened to consume him, sleep was elusive. He saw a doctor who talked him through some relaxation techniques, but they were only so helpful. Despite everything, he somehow managed to finish high school.

The following year was rough. Jama saw his friends enjoying the first rush of adulthood, embarking on careers or tertiary study, while his own future was in limbo. For about three months he held down a job with a caravan-building business in Campbellfield, only to ditch it as the shadow of his impending court case loomed.

At the start of 2008, he pulled himself together yet again, landing a full-time job in nearby Thomastown with a company that made carton boxes. On Saturdays he worked at a Somali restaurant near his home. Jama would tell his barrister that he rarely went out during this period because he wanted to avoid any further trouble.

Part of Jama's bail conditions required him to report to Preston police station. In an interview with *Age* journalist Liz Porter in 2010, nearly a year after his vindication, Jama related an incident that occurred on one of these visits to the station. An officer at the desk quipped, 'Oh, you're the rapist.' Jama had felt his face burn with shame.

He was ashamed. Most young men would feel ashamed at being labelled a rapist. Especially if they were nothing of the sort. But the noun, *shame*, is declarative, heavy as stone. I wondered if Jama himself used that word when he described the incident to the journalist. These days you so rarely hear young men speak of *shame*. In Somali circles, on the other hand, I heard the word often, usually as the flipside of that other antique and rather exotic concept, *honour*. Family honour, clan honour. Somalis, I was told by more than one person, sometimes twisted the truth about seemingly trivial matters, especially when speaking with outsiders who wouldn't know any different, for reasons of 'convoluted family politics'.

Personal honour. An historian told me about the time he travelled in northern Somalia with three battle-hardened bodyguards who he later found out were being paid a mere $50 a month to protect him. 'And I said, "Are you prepared to die for $50?" And they said, "Well, $40 goes back to our family, we keep $10, but we will die before you, or else what would be left for us, what would we do? The *shame* would be too great." It's the attitude I have met in poor people before,' the historian explained, 'the belief that all you have is your integrity.'

'They are very private people and rape is something so *shameful*,' one friend of the Jama family explained to me. I had found a handful of people who knew the Jamas and were willing to talk; all my enquiries led back to the same handful of people. The first this friend had heard of Jama's strife was in media reports of the trial. 'The family didn't want the matter to leave the backyard,' he said.

Another friend insisted: 'We knew *nothing*, nothing until after the conviction.'

It appeared the family kept quiet about the charges. For shame, for honour, for convoluted family politics. It is unclear whether anyone beyond immediate kin was allowed to know the trial was pending.

Astonishingly, the Jamas and Osman scraped together and borrowed almost $30,000 for the boy's defence.

One Friday morning I met my Somali friend and cultural interpreter, Yusuf, for coffee at the Paris End of Collins Street. True to form, he immediately handed over a wad of academic articles and reports about the Somali community. Yusuf's voice is lilting and warm. His face is small and bony, his frame slight. Often he appears to be swimming inside his suit jackets. Though once when I saw him in traditional African dress—a long caftan-style shirt, with emerald green and gold embroidery, and matching pants and cap—he looked so resplendent and regal that it startled me.

I had met Yusuf years ago, while he was completing a PhD on the aspirations and achievements of Somali youth in Australia, the UK and the United States. His views are unorthodox. For instance, he blames a generous social welfare system for contributing to a deeper sense of alienation among young Somalis in Australia and the UK, compared with their peers in the US. He says Somalis in their new lands must resist adopting a 'victim mentality'.

'And I'm a poet, too,' Yusuf told me early in our friendship.

In Somalia, where the national tongue only became a written language in 1972 and the oral tradition is strong, men of verse enjoy significant prestige. I had read some of Yusuf's poetry; recordings of his time spent in Maribyrnong detention centre, and numerous idealised tributes to the courage and wisdom of Somali women: 'Admirable Girls!', 'Honourable Somali Woman!', 'Proud Sisters!', 'Stand Up!', 'Unite!'

On this morning he nodded, tight faced, through my bleakly prosaic narrative of the Farah Jama case. He was suffering a toothache, a fact he only divulged as we were leaving.

'What you have to bear in mind, Julie,' he said, after I'd wrapped up, 'is that anything to do with sexual matters is taboo. That's one thing. Another thing to bear in mind is that Somalis, especially the older generation, spent time under a dictatorship [of General Barre] and are very suspicious of the authorities and the police.'

In a paper published in 2007, a Canadian-Somali sociologist, Cawo Mohamed Abdi, analyses the response to rape in traditional society:

> Rape in Somali culture is very stigmatising. Prior to the [Somali civil] war it was rare and severely condemned, making group or clan relations very tense when it occurred. Women's virginity was highly valued, and violating their honour was considered scandalous. With the war and the collapse of law and order, group relations and societal norms were turned upside down.[1]

Rape became a tool of the clan warriors; women were forced into marriage. In a remote refugee camp in Kenya, local bandits had reportedly preyed on women when they were out collecting firewood. As a response, women started to dress more conservatively. They wore long-johns or trousers under their robes because they were harder to rip off, and also because they were believed to more strongly emphasise chastity. The veil too became a mark of purity and good character. Rape was too shameful to speak of, and yet so ubiquitous it shaped the dress codes of everyday.

What might Jama's mother have understood about the darker impulses of men, of the shocking accusation that had shattered her family's hard-earned peace? I thought of someone who could shed at least some light. She was Zeinab Mohamud,

---

[1] 'Convergence of Civil War and the Religious Right: Reimagining Somali Women', *Signs: Journal of Women in Culture and Society 2007*, vol. 33, no 1.

a community development worker at Melbourne's Royal Women's Hospital, whose role includes counselling families with newborn girls against female circumcision. I met her years ago and was impressed with her candour. At the time she said that if I was ever around her neighbourhood in West Melbourne I ought to drop by and say hello.

By the time I contacted her in 2011, she had forgotten both me and the offer, but agreed to a meeting all the same. In the meantime she had advanced in her pursuit of the Great Australian Dream and shifted from the inner city to a new housing development in Melbourne's outer west. I'd need a latest edition road map to find her house in Point Cook, she said.

On the day of our meeting, I drove down a long, monotonous road and turned down a series of residential streets to arrive at her cul de sac. At 11 am all was quiet; the city's urban frontier as always, serene and inscrutable. Zeinab, a forty-year-old mother of five, greeted me in black pants and a leopard-print blue and brown shirt. A large shawl, cream with gold sequins, was draped around her shoulders and chest; a headscarf, black with white flowers, was tied loosely at the back to reveal hoop earrings. Her full face broke easily into a smile. As we headed to the lounge, she gestured for me to remove my shoes. The soft carpet felt soothing under my feet. The room was sparingly furnished with a couch and armchairs decorated with elaborate gold-trimmed upholstery in a Baroque–meets–Arabian Nights' style.

We talked at first about female circumcision, a discussion

that served as a grim but useful prologue. The practice was almost universal in Somalia, Zeinab explained, 'part of the psyche'. She said women born before the 1980s were likely to have undergone infibulation, the most extreme and harmful form of mutilation: the clitoris and some or all of the genital lips are cut away and the raw surfaces stitched together to cover the urethra and most of the vagina. Urine collects under the folds and drips out, slowly. During childbirth the woman is simply snipped open again along the seam. Many girls had it done at ages eleven or twelve in the refugee camps in Kenya, often without anaesthetic. A wave of discomfort passed over Zeinab's face. She admitted to only seeing the light herself after influential men in her life managed to convince her that the practice had no religious basis.

'My husband, who spent four years in Saudi Arabia, said they don't do it there. It has nothing to do with Islam!'

I resisted a barb about Saudi Arabia being held up as a model of enlightenment. Thankfully, Zeinab's Road to Mecca conversion came in time to spare her own daughters.

After a short while she prepared tea with cinnamon and cardamom pods. And then I asked her about rape and the Somali civil war. She related to me a memory, taking the long route because I asked her to—it didn't seem right to cherry pick for relevance.

So I heard about the 'Big Bang Sunday' in 1990 in Mogadishu. About the men who appeared suddenly with guns. About the militia looting the police station, and the shelling in the early hours. About her escape on foot in the middle of the night, as the stray bullets flew and as the bodies piled up at the roadside. About how her sister finally caught up with them but not before the thugs had beaten her black and blue. 'And then someone will come from our area and they would say, "Do you know so-and-so? He was shot".' About the forty-three people, most of them children, squeezed into a fishing vessel that almost ran aground in shallow, stinking waters. About how they took refuge in a house in the country's south. The house had a cistern, an underground storage container for rainwater, secured with a grille. They drained the water, dried the floor and hid there, beneath the metal cover, on 'bad nights'.

'On bad nights,' Zeinab said, 'in the surrounding houses, people would break in and steal … and rape. You can hear the cries, you can hear the begging, you can hear every nighttime, "Oh God, help me!"'

She hesitated a moment.

'Some of them had undergone the infibulation.' These men were 'trying to rape a woman who'd been closed up'.

We sipped the tea.

Hours passed. We talked generally about the challenges facing the younger generation, about the young Somali men caught between the piety of their parents and the temptations of a secular society.

'And you know,' Zeinab continued, 'now we actually have some wild Somali girls, too.'

According to Zeinab, these girls from the suburbs head out veiled and modestly dressed. Once they hit town, headscarves come off, miniskirts come on and booze comes out.

She smiled wryly. 'And so when the girls are wild, some mothers are saying, "See, had we circumcised them, none of this would have happened!"'

The neighbourhood was still quiet when I left. It still had that unfinished, accidental look. The long drive home came as a relief. I contemplated journeys: the epic journeys from danger to safety, and the uneven, invisible and quietly astonishing journeys that end with a change of mind.

I returned to the same section of the transcript that continued to trouble me: Osman is asked by Jama's counsel whether the youth had trouble integrating, to which he replies, 'I believe Farah is a very nice boy who don't talk too much. He keeps always quiet.' The answer is obviously a non-sequitur, but after several readings, what really struck me was the description of Jama: *a very nice boy who keeps always quiet, who don't talk too much.*

The description was troubling because common sense dictated that Jama, having been charged with rape, needed to start talking. Even if those closest to him were too crippled by shame to ask the right questions, he still needed to give some answers. Even if it meant talking *too much.*

To what extent had this *very nice boy* been frank with his father, his mother, his siblings, with Osman, and most critically with his lawyers? Indeed, I wondered if Jama had even managed to confer privately with his own barrister. I wondered if his relatives had spoken openly between themselves. Had they mulled over the contradictions, brainstormed the possibilities? Did Jama's father know everything Osman knew? Perhaps some matters were deemed too *shameful* to share with the mother, in the same way men find it too shameful to speak of the flight from Kenya, of the children they left behind. In the same way only a woman could ask another woman about the unspeakable.

When I told a middle-aged Somali woman about Jama and the young woman from the pool hall and the allegation of forced oral sex, she screwed up her face in distaste and sympathy for the parents.

'It [oral sex] is disgusting, it is un-Islamic,' she explained. 'You would feel like this child let you down.'

She said the clerics needed to take more responsibility, to guide Somali youth. The young men were watching pornography, absorbing sexualised messages from the mainstream. Muslims were forbidden from engaging in fellatio or anal sex, she insisted. Only vaginal sex with one's partner in marriage was permitted.

'We don't even have a word for oral sex in our language.'

I found this almost impossible to believe, however sincere my informant. On the other hand, perhaps a devout woman of a certain age was unlikely to have heard it. And if a young man wanted to tell his Somali-speaking parents about having had oral sex with a girl in a car, how would he even find the words?

In order to be sure, I persisted with the questions over many months. The answers, for obvious reasons though, were pure hearsay. I asked an acquaintance of the Jamas whether Farah's mother knew how his DNA came to be on the police database in the first place. The acquaintance said someone in their circle had asked the mother precisely this question, only to receive a vague answer about Jama and two other boys having been involved in 'a fight at the pool'.

'A fight at the pool?' I gasped at the absurdity. 'Did she mean a *swimming* pool?'

'I think so, yes.'

What was I to make of this? Had Jama orchestrated a game of broken telephone to spare his mother the truth? Thus, pool hall became swimming pool and a contested allegation about forced oral sex was syncopated and distorted to 'a fight'. Or had his mother known all the sordid facts but kept them close lest her family become the subject of shameful gossip? The latter proposition was of course possible, but the more I learned, the more doubtful it seemed. And yet, had Jama related every detail about that eventful weekend of 14 and 15 July 2006, after which he first became known to police, had he talked about it over and over, dwelling on all the bizarre, baffling and strangely synchronous aspects of the mess in which he found himself, then *surely* someone would have eventually thought to go searching for the missing piece of the puzzle?

At almost every juncture I leaned to the conclusion that Jama didn't talk too much and perhaps didn't talk much at all.

I went to see a Somali man who talked freely, if anonymously, about secrets and lies and taboos and convoluted family politics. We met in a chilly office alongside a tower of commission flats.

'You know some people in the Somali community say that I am not on their side,' the man said, piles of documents stacked high around him.

'They see me as against them, but I'm not against them, I just want to understand, I want to question. And do you know why I am this way? It is because I was an interpreter and interpreters are different because we see into people's lives. Sometimes when they are saying something we know that they are not telling the truth, and hearing that again and again will put you in the situation where you question everything.

'… I interpreted for everyone: the Office of Housing, Immigration, the police, many times. This is the baggage that lies have in our profession. And when I started asking questions [of people] about immigration or housing or whatever, and would have to then go back again and ask more questions, by then they say, "OK, fuck off …"'

He trailed off. I asked him if people tended to tell their own families the truth.

'Let me tell you a story.' He launched into the case of a teenage runaway, a girl, who nevertheless kept in regular contact with her mother. The girl's father was worried sick, but still the mother refused to divulge her knowledge and put his mind at rest.

'And I'll give you another example. I know of families

where someone is in hospital, seriously sick. And a close relative, say a brother or sister, will ring up and ask the man, "How's the family? How is your wife?" And the man will say that she is okay, she's fine. So the person won't tell their own brother or sister about their wife being sick with a mental illness.

'If you have a mental illness back home, then God help you. There are many matters that are taboo. As we speak, there are Africans in prison and if you go and ask the mothers where are they, they will say, "Holidaying in Somalia". Taboos, clans … people are scared that the truth will get around and be used against them.'

Question marks pocked my notebook. Would someone who told me something later regret their honesty and try to deny it? Was someone really someone else's uncle or cousin? Did someone have an ulterior motive in relating that story? People who criticised the secrecy of others were shown to be themselves secretive. It was around this time that I began to hesitate and doubt, to lose my footing.

In November 2011, I went to an inner-city gallery to hear a talk by an exhibiting Somali artist, Nadia Faragaab, a young woman critical of her community's taboos. I had been in her company once before, at the graduation ceremony at Parliament House, where she had stood out for being virtually the only female without a head covering.

'That takes courage,' a Somali woman beside me had murmured, pointing to Nadia and her riot of reddish-brown curls.

This afternoon her hair was tied back with a clip. She wore a blue T-shirt and jeans. Her exhibition, 'Kronologies', explored Somali identity through fabrics, installations and a plundering of digital images from the mass media; everything from masked jihadists to the Somali soccer team. Again, the Somali soccer team.

In one room stood a faceless mannequin draped in a black, Saudi-style *jilbaab*, from under which peeped the hem of a lighter, less modest dress, the kind Somali women used to wear before the civil war. In an adjacent room, Nadia had assembled an idealised Somali living-room, trying to imagine domestic life, had war and displacement never happened. She married Africa and the West, the coffee table bearing a traditional head-rest or 'pillow', a golden metallic teapot and a glossy 'African Vogue' with a glamorous, scantily dressed woman on the cover. In the corner, an incense of sugar and frankincense gave off a piquant, musky fragrance. It was the Somali heartache with which I had become all too familiar. *What could have been, what should have been, homelands, fantasy lands.*

During her artist's talk, Nadia's words seemed to tumble out, her passion frenetic, her mind sharp as a sword. A passerby once called her a 'filthy nigger', and you know what she did? She turned around and started following him! She stalked him, that's what! The crowd was in stitches. A veteran Somali activist gave a rousing speech from the floor. He spoke of his time in Britain during the Brixton riots in the 1980s; cops harassed him, skinheads broke his legs. Just as second-generation blacks had their political awakening then, so too a young generation of Africans here were beginning to take up the fight against racism! Nadia was proud of her Somali past, but still figuring out how best to preserve it. She wanted more debate within the community, '… about the things we don't discuss … sexuality, alcohol, the *jilbaab* …' She flung her arm at the draped mannequin.

'This garment is such a recent thing … why don't we talk about that?! You know, there is a Somali saying that when you hide and conceal things, they fester and stink.'

The veteran activist nodded in furious agreement. A veiled woman in the audience raised her eyebrows and hunched her shoulders, looking surprised and unsure. The veteran activist rose again to his feet.

'Somalis must resist perpetuating a "fossilised" version of their culture!'

It was a humid day, I was cross-legged on the floor. A woman gestured at me to move away from the wall. I had been leaning against an exhibit without realising. The claustrophobia came on suddenly. Tightness in my throat, mild panic welling up inside. I longed to flee the gallery.

The incense wafting in from the next room had become pungent and oppressive, festering and stinking.

Chapter 12

In a previous life, about fifteen years ago, I worked as a solicitor. Much of the daily grind has since blurred, but I can still vividly remember the immersive pleasure of a long court case. For those days or weeks all the world was a courtroom. Sitting opposite counsel at the bar table, required to do little more than make the occasional note or fumble for the odd document, I would soak up the spectacle. The twists and turns of evidence, the witnesses stammering in the box, the barristers perspiring under their wigs and robes as they persuaded and blustered, sparred and seduced. For me it was as suspenseful as a sporting match.

Sadly, I wasn't present for any part of the six-day County Court trial of *The Queen vs Farah Abdulkadir Jama,* which commenced before Judge Paul Lacava on Monday 14 July 2008, just one day shy of two years since Maria was found on the toilet floor. I instead experienced the Jama trial through the transcript of proceedings, an intriguing, mind-numbing and intensely frustrating document of more than five hundred pages. While denied the frisson and charge of a courtroom in which a man's liberty was at stake, I did have the unfair advantage of hindsight, which gave the proceedings an absurdist quality. It felt as if I were watching the action unfold under water.

Barrister George Slim appeared for the Prosecution. He came to this trial with more than thirty-five years' experience, and what seemed to me an old-school sensibility. Failing to find even an email address on his website, I sent him a formal letter. He responded likewise with a note written in an elegant, sloping hand on unlined white paper, thanking me for my letter, but advising he would be unavailable for interview. The gentlemanly 'Thank you' made me warm to him. A colleague of Slim's from the bar described him as 'a cunning and effective prosecutor'.

The firm of solicitors Michael J. Gleeson & Associates represented Jama, along with the same barrister who had appeared for him at the committal, Ian Crisp. A website for 'Ian Crisp Criminal Defence Lawyer' showed a round-faced man with even features and soft white hair trimmed neatly above the ears and combed flat to one side. He wore a black suit with a white shirt and red patterned tie. A white handkerchief sprouted from his breast pocket. The website itself went on to make a number of intemperate claims about Crisp's professional track record, including an assertion he'd represented clients from *all* ethnic communities (of which he listed 'Arabic' as one, even though it's strictly speaking a language and not a community) and that he utilises his years of experience in criminal law to 'obtain the desired result for each and every one of his clients', which on any analysis is a pitch as vague as it is incautious.

Who decides what the 'desired result' might entail—Crisp or his client?

A series of phone calls with Crisp was enough to convince me the site did not do justice to the man. He was unfailingly courteous, even when I said or wrote something that riled and hurt him. Through our strained and halting and invariably circular conversations, I sensed a caring and careful professional, upset at the travesty his client suffered, if understandably reticent about conceding to a journalist how his own failures helped bring it about. Because there was one thing I could readily wager: Crisp fell short of 'the desired result' for a young African who in July 2008 faced trial on one count of rape.

As for Judge Lacava, I stumbled on a profile that was read out at his official welcome to the bench. The child of a working-class family, Lacava took labouring jobs to put himself through university. Though possessed of a strong social conscience, he was also admired for his 'mature ease' with all kinds of people, including colleagues who went fox hunting in the UK with the Duke of Edinburgh. Perhaps the most significant part of the welcome speech was its date: 5 June 2008. The Farah Jama trial was only his third case.

When you read for dramatic irony (and how could I not?) the marginal action in a courtroom—the casual banter between judge and barristers, the asides, the routine housekeeping matters—is thrust into centre stage. During the accused's arraignment, for instance, Judge Lacava made a polite query about the proper pronunciation of 'Jama'.

And I noted that on day two of trial when the prosecutor flagged the possibility of delay—the toxicologist couldn't give evidence because he was sick and the audio of Jama's police interview was still being edited—Slim was most apologetic, confiding in the judge, 'I'm just worrying about the climate of the times'.

I remembered a similar phrase had been used by Detective Karen Porter's supervisor, Neil Beeson, in his email to police forensics: '*In the current climate* I need to be able to discount the possibility of cross contamination …' Was this the political context to Jama's ordeal? The intense pressure felt by bureaucrats and professionals to avoid errors and to get results, and get them fast?

I also noted how Crisp, Jama's counsel, told the judge that the trial would be relatively short. In relation to the DNA evidence against the accused, the Defence was going to argue 'an irregularity, an anomaly'. To which the judge asked, 'Is it contamination?'

'No,' replied Jama's counsel, 'it's not contamination.'

The jury was empanelled, the Defence and Prosecution made brief opening statements and by mid-afternoon the Crown called its first witness, Maria. Having read the Victim Impact Statement she would present to the judge at the subsequent sentencing hearing, I knew something of Maria's emotional state as she stepped into the witness box.

In the aftermath of her traumatic experience in the nightclub, Maria's confidence withered and her world contracted. No longer secure in the company of Sophie and Alex, she broke off contact with them. (Even though, as Sophie herself would tell the court, the pair had hung round the club until one o'clock in the morning trying to find her.) Maria's family provided little succour. They blamed her. She mourned her lost sense of self. She was cast into a lonely, secret exile.

'I left the nightclub that night, in an ambulance, having lost my memory of most of the night, my dignity and nearly my life,' she wrote. 'I was violated in a most reprehensible way and preyed upon by another individual. I have felt such shame, rage and unrelenting guilt, that I do not think it will ever leave me.'

She thought of herself, she said in her statement, as an independent and capable woman, fiercely in control of her life. Now she struggled to maintain her work schedule, she avoided social functions. Sometimes she cried herself to sleep. Other times she tore through the streets in the dead of night, watching the speedometer climb.

'I distrust most people, but especially men,' Maria confessed. 'I have refused getting into taxis when [the] driver was of the dark persuasion.'

'Of the dark persuasion,' was as awkward as it was revealing. Had Maria's attacker been Caucasian would she likewise have avoided drivers of the 'pale persuasion'? Not that I judged Maria for seeing Farah Jama in every African cab driver. It probably pained her to succumb to such base prejudice. Trauma warps the mind.

'I didn't think of myself as naive—if this could happen to me, then it could happen to anybody else,' she concluded. 'The court proceedings have not been easy for me but I needed to do this for myself and to get some closure and, hopefully, to protect the rights of other women in the community.'

Her statement was predictably sad. I felt a cascade of sympathy. Then almost immediately that sympathy began wrestling bafflement and irritation. She was a respected professional, who held a position of trust and responsibility. She was also in her late forties. So why in God's name had she been pre-loading in the car like a teenager? A bipolar woman skating close to the edge, flirting with abandonment; a self-declared control freak daring herself to lose control.

Of course, I had had my fair share of reckless nights, driven by grief or disappointment or sheer boredom to all but break out of my skin. I had been there, sure. But in my teens or twenties. Maria was nearly fifty, for crying out loud, and hardly in perfect health! Where was her judgment? As Maria confirmed from the witness box, for the past twelve years she had been taking Tegretol for her bipolar condition, and two other prescription drugs, one of them for about four years, for other medical conditions. Yet, she told the prosecutor, she could still drink 'within the limitation'.

For all my bafflement and irritation, I applauded Maria's strength. Her fortitude was again on impressive display. As in the committal hearing, she chose to give evidence in open court even though recently enacted laws gave complainants the automatic right to do so by remote facility. I assumed she was motivated by a wish to deny her alleged attacker any satisfaction he might gain from seeing her shrivel and hide. She wanted no screen placed between her and the accused, and needed no support person to sit beside her. She wanted none of it.

Maria's evidence was clear and insistent and forthright. She gave a consistent account of her patchy recollection of the night. She told the court what she ate, what she wore and approximately how much she drank. The prosecutor asked, 'I presume, like most of us, you've had the experience of being drunk on occasions?' Maria said indeed she had, but had never before passed out after a few glasses of Frangelico.

Occasionally, her narration wobbled on an odd turn of phrase, such as when she described walking to a standing table 'ostensibly for the purpose of lighting my cigarette'. Slim had to clarify her meaning, but I felt a warm burst of her personality. She recounted chatting with the two men, then waking on the floor with pain in her armpits, 'pain in my chest over my sternum—'.

'Your sternum is what—, said Slim.

'My chest bone, here.'

'Between your breasts?'

'Yes.'

And Maria stood firm even as Slim, the prosecutor, ever apologetic, dipped into her sex life.

'I have to ask you these questions,' he explained, 'because they're relevant or could be relevant.'

Before that Saturday night, when had she last engaged in sexual activity?

About a week earlier, Maria responded, with her then boyfriend. It had been foreplay only. No penetration or ejaculation.

'Was it then some time since you'd had any sexual intercourse in the sense of penetration of your vagina?'

'Some considerable time, yes.'

'Did you know anybody around that time by the name of Farah Jama?'

'No, I did not.'

'Have you ever heard the name before?'

'No, I had not.'

'Did you know or see the gentleman in the dock?'

'No.'

'Did you give anybody that night permission to sexually touch you in any way, or do anything sexual to you?'

'No, I did not.'

※

Among exhibits tendered by the prosecution was a book of photographs of Maria. She wears a white hospital gown and shell-shocked expression. The hair she had 'styled down' the night before hangs limp around her shoulders. In one photo she gazes dull-eyed at the camera, in another she twists and stretches her neck, as if striking a pose, to highlight the bruises on her skin. She looks vulnerable and bereft.

※

She faced up gamely to Crisp's cross-examination. No, she hadn't seen any 'dark-skinned' men at the venue. She suspected somebody in the club might have had the opportunity to tamper with her second drink, but couldn't be sure. Her last memory was of being in the company of a man who was a bit odd, 'a bit sleazy,' yes, those were her words. And yes it was crowded, and yes the toilets where she had later been found were 'some distance' away. And no, she couldn't be sure that someone had had sex with her that night.

The nightclub witnesses, the supervisor, Stephanie Johnstone and two security guards passed through the witness box without fireworks. Yet, if the truth was anywhere in that courtroom, it lay buried in the apparently uncontentious recollections of these three.

Johnstone, who had since left the hospitality industry altogether, once again exhausted her memory of that night. The alert from the security guard at 10.50 pm, the leg lolling out from beneath the locked cubicle, Maria slumped on the floor with her button and zip undone, the estimated six hundred to eight hundred patrons at the venue, the guards carrying Maria's 'dead weight' from the toilets to the backstage area, a distance of about ten metres. And the tape on the floor in the band room?

'There's tape everywhere,' Johnstone said. 'We use that to tape down the cords for the bands.'

'Was there any tape on the female that you noticed?'

'Not that I knew of.'

While Maria was being carried, her pants slid down 'slightly, just a little bit, probably half way down, just to the hip'. Her buttocks were barely visible. Yes, they could have come into contact with the carpet. And yes, the bruises could also have occurred then.

Security guards, Mikayil Mohammed Umar, a.k.a. 'Kyle' and Chalimi 'Charlie' Cosan, explained how they had carried Maria from the toilet cubicle to the band room.

'Well, we,' said Umar, 'pretty much just one arm each, so you know, general, under the arm and then carried her out.'

He didn't exactly see Maria's pants come down, but he knew they were down because he was the one who covered her with a curtain.

Cosan reckoned three of them had carried her motionless body to the band room. He recalled a third security guard 'known as Ash' who had also helped. Yes, there had been three of them, maybe even four. He remembered having to hold her tightly so she wouldn't slip.

So it took at least three men to haul the unconscious Maria from the toilets to the band room. Yet the Prosecution was implicitly asking the jury to believe Jama had single-handedly manoeuvred the unconscious woman across the packed nightclub to the toilets, leapt over the cubicle wall and vanished into the night, all without being seen.

Did the jury think, well, a dark-skinned man *could* prowl about under camouflage of darkness? Might they have accepted the simple explanation for the Hitchcockian details—the bruises, the pants around the hips, (buttocks 'barely' visible), the duct tape? Could they have seen past

Jama, or was he always there; a shadowy menace lurking somewhere off-camera?

The Prosecution raced through batches of witnesses. Forensic physician Dr Janet Towns had documented the bruising on Maria's inner thighs about ten days after the incident. Various 'continuity' witnesses were able to verify the safe passage of Maria's samples from the hospital to the lab. A toxicologist testified on the results of Maria's urine screen, and answered questions about GHB, an illicit drug known as Fantasy or Grievous Bodily Harm, which 'has been used in drug facilitated sexual assault cases'—and which was not detected in this case. Jama's counsel asked him whether combining the drug Tegretol with alcohol could result in blackouts. The toxicologist replied that if enough alcohol was consumed then yes, it could.

Nicola Cunningham, the forensic medical officer who examined Maria at the Austin hospital, was described to me as a stylish brunette who wears her long hair in a ponytail. She has a habit of starting her sentences with 'So …' as in, 'So, the endocervical region is the region where it's the opening to the neck of the womb' and 'So a swab … actually looks like an elongated cotton bud'. The habit suggested to me a methodical mind.

She gave evidence about Maria's bruises. The yellow ones must have pre-dated the incident as they were at least eighteen hours old, Cunningham said, but the red or blue or purple ones could have occurred on the night. The cluster of bruises under Maria's armpit resembled fingertip bruising, 'which means they could have occurred from a forceful grasp before being lifted'. It was Cunningham's qualifications that struck me as most interesting. In the ten years since her graduation she had worked as a toxicology registrar, an emergency registrar in the Women's Hospital and a forensic registrar for the Victorian Institute of Forensic Medicine. I was inclined to see someone tough, ambitious and capable—a woman who set exacting standards for herself, as women so often do.

'Members of the jury, as you can see the case is rattling along pretty quickly,' noted Judge Lacava. A slide projector was being set up. It was after 3 pm, late in the court day, when forensic biologist Deborah Scott stepped into the box. She was the twelfth witness of that day and the most important from the Prosecution's point of view. After all, it was Scott who would interpret the fateful evidence, the only evidence, on which the Crown hoped to nail Farah Jama.

Chapter 13

'What is DNA?' said Deborah Scott.

'Well, DNA stands for deoxyribonucleic acid. It's a complex chemical that contains all of the information that determines our inheritable characteristics. It is inherited from our parents, half from our mother and half from our father. Next slide.

'DNA is found in most cells within the human body such as blood, skin or semen. It is the same throughout your body. The DNA in skin cells will be the same as the DNA in your saliva. Next slide.'

Slim, the prosecutor, kept her on an even keel, reeling her in when she rushed ahead, smoothing over her clumsy sentences, clarity his beacon.

'A DNA typing result can indicate whether the material has originated from a male or a female … Next slide.

'DNA can be transferred from person to person or from person to place, or person to item. Another example could be semen being transferred from one person to another person during sexual intercourse.'

Half an hour passed before Slim reached 'a convenient place to stop'. The jurors were sent home that afternoon with a gentle warning from the judge. While they may have seen TV references to DNA, the Judge said, the subject was complex for people without scientific backgrounds and it was crucial they not leap to conclusions about the case.

The following morning, Judge Lacava told Slim and Crisp he'd been doing a lot of reading around DNA. He thought it a good idea to give the jury a hard copy of Scott's PowerPoint presentation, because 'there's no point talking about DNA if you don't know what the hell it is'. The newly-minted judge was nothing if not conscientious. But under the influence of both learned counsel, he lost sight of the bigger picture as he set about conquering mountains of scientific detail. He failed to see the crude belief that dictated so much of the action in his courtroom.

Scott stepped back into the witness box. The prosecutor asked her if 'strict procedures' existed in the police lab to guard against contamination. Yes, she said. Not only were there strict procedures to prevent contamination, but also to detect if it had occurred. She elaborated with a precision that led me to believe that she delivered the lines often.

The lab was accredited by the national testing authority. Scientists wore protective clothing. There were never two exhibits on a bench at the same time. After each exhibit the benches were cleaned and the blotting paper changed. Exhibits from the same case were examined at different areas within the laboratory. Positive and negative controls had to be run before recording a test result. The transfer of materials from one tube to another was always witnessed and verified. Staff were themselves DNA profiled to ensure they didn't inadvertently contaminate samples. Whenever she signed off on a report, a second biologist had to back her findings.

In this case, Scott wound up, there was no evidence that any contamination had occurred.

Slim carried the jury on a tide of inevitability.

'The male seed was found on one of Maria's cervical slides, yes?'

'Correct,' said Scott.

The corresponding swabs, she explained, revealed a mixed DNA profile, which originated from at least two individuals. The smaller component of the mixture matched the profile of Maria. This was not surprising given they were talking about the victim's vagina. As for the major component of the DNA mixture, it matched the DNA profile of Farah Jama, which meant he could not be excluded as the source.

To be more precise, the chances of the DNA on the swabs having originated from a random Australian male, who just happened to share Jama's profile, were probably one in 800 billion, and anywhere between 45 billion to 14 trillion. The odds were similarly astronomical when, for the sake of 'rigour', she substituted the random Australian with a random Somali. 'So, in my opinion,' Scott concluded, 'in the absence of other information, the results presented, provide extremely strong support for the proposition that the major component of the DNA mixture obtained from the swabs came from Farah Jama.'

All the same, the jury put up admirable resistance to Slim. They asked questions. Did Scott know how many DNA samples had been contaminated since the national accreditation body came into existence? No, not off the top of her head. And what was the size and origin of the Somali database used for the statistical analysis? There were ninety-six unrelated individuals, gathered from a study that had been published in 2004 in the International Congress Series.

After a mid-morning break, Jama's counsel, Crisp, embarked on his cross-examination of Scott. Alas, he persistently failed to match Slim's flair for drama and storytelling. Earlier in the trial, for instance, the prosecutor managed to leave the jury on a cliffhanger when the court adjourned for the day. Maria had just said, '… and the next thing I knew I was in an ambulance', when Slim suggested that might be a convenient time to stop. And Slim invariably began his cross-examination of a witness with a sharp or confrontational question.

By contrast, Crisp's first question to the forensic biologist was in the nature of an afterthought, a clarification. The sentence began with an 'And'.

'And just in case this is asked,' Crisp said, 'how large was the database that you used in relation to the Australian population?'

After the afterthought came his intended opening. Crisp

recounted that when Scott had said the lab results supported the proposition that the DNA came from Farah Jama, she qualified her conclusions with the phrase, 'in the absence of other information'.

'Do you remember saying that?'

'Yes,' Scott replied.

'What did you mean by that?'

'In the absence of other information,' Scott repeated, 'which may be other evidence that you have been presented with that I'm unaware of.'

Crisp's question was well-aimed, but it lacked firepower. He had no 'other evidence' to unleash. And in the absence of any other expert evidence to attack the DNA results, to attack the fundamental and fundamentally flawed assumption almost everyone had drawn from those results, Crisp's only hope was to attempt to poke holes in the data. He had prepared for the task before trial by seeking some guidance in a phone call to a La Trobe University geneticist, and was plainly undaunted by detail. But while at committal he had circled maddeningly close to the salient clues, this time he dragged the jury straight into the thicket and left them there.

He challenged Scott about the one sperm with its tail intact that she detected on the slide. A sperm with a tail could have survived in Maria's vagina for longer than 48 hours after intercourse, couldn't it?

'I suggest that from a scientific point of view you can't conclusively rule that out,' Crisp insisted. Scott was emphatic. No, she would not expect sperm with tails to survive any longer than 48 hours. She had never seen sperm with tails survive longer than 48 hours. I found the question perplexing: Maria had already said that before the fateful Saturday night she had not been sexually active for some time.

Crisp hammered the presence of 'anomalies' in the DNA profiling. He referred jurors to a summary table of DNA results. He directed them across and down the table so they could locate various sets of numbers and letters and other markings that pertained to the swab taken from Maria's cervix.

He interrogated Scott about the appearance of extra 'peaks' on the electropherogram. Didn't these 'peaks' suggest there were more patterns, more 'alleles' as they're called, on the DNA strand apart from those that belonged to Jama and Maria? Certainly not, Scott insisted, over and over. What Crisp was calling a 'peak' was simply a 'stutter', an irregularity or hiccup that occurs during the process of amplification in laboratories the world over.

Again and again Crisp challenged her about these 'peaks' that she insisted were 'stutters'. And then came a jolt. Crisp was pressing Scott. But *if* one of those peaks at one of those sites on the DNA strand *was* real, Crisp persisted, then it wouldn't match the profile of either Maria or Jama, would it? And then surely, Crisp continued, she couldn't rule out a contribution from a *third person*?

An icy thought crept up on me. For a brief moment, I followed Crisp's desperate logic to its ultimate conclusion. Could it be true? Could the sample from Maria's cervix have contained traces of a third person? My mind grabbed at outlandish scenarios. Did the jurors also experience a moment's turbulence? I wondered if Crisp's cross-examination forced at least some of them to fleetingly consider whether Maria might have been raped by not just one man, but two.

Chapter 14

Four days into the trial, the jury was played the audio recording of Jama's police interview that took place nearly eighteen months earlier at the Doncaster Criminal Investigation Unit. The recording had been edited to remove discussion of the pool hall incident that occurred the night before the Doncaster incident. All that remained from this section of the interview was a dangling reference to 'a pool hall in Reservoir'. The interview took place at 8.59 am on Tuesday, 14 November 2006, four months after Maria's nightclub ordeal, with Detective Senior Constable Karen Porter and a male officer. Porter spoke in slow, measured tones, scrupulously patient. Jama's answers came in a faint, sometimes wavering, voice. Porter confirmed for the record that the police officers had gone to Jama's house at ten to eight that morning. They spoke to him in the presence of his mother, father and sisters. They asked him if he'd ever been to Hotel Shoppingtown in Doncaster. He said he hadn't, he said he'd never even been to the suburb of Doncaster. The officers told him he was under arrest.

'Now on the way back to the police station,' Porter continued, 'when we were in the car, I pointed out the shopping centre. Remember I said, "On the left there is the Doncaster Shopping Centre?" And what did you tell me?'

'Never s…take a s…step in there and that I don't know where it is,' stammered Jama. 'Never been there my whole life.'

I felt the familiar rush of protectiveness towards him. The immaturity accentuated his vulnerability. 'Never been there in my whole life'—the childishness of the phrase deepened the sense of pathos. It was the way my eight-year-old speaks. 'Never, ever, never in my whole wide life …'

He uttered the phrase over and over as the detectives again and again challenged him on his never having been to Doncaster. In the process, the police mapped the geography of his 'whole life'. From Somalia to Kenya, to New Zealand to Australia, to Carlton, where the family first lived on arrival in Melbourne, to Preston, to Thomastown and back to Preston.

Asked about his work, Jama said he'd had casual jobs in Preston and Thornbury, construction among them, and that he currently worked for his uncle in the Flemington restaurant. Did he own a credit or debit card? No, he did not. Did he have a bank account? No.

So what did he do with his cash earnings from the restaurant? He 'just put 'em somewhere in the house'. He saved the money. He bought a car with his mother's help.

So the money didn't go in the bank at all? No.

✥

'Okay,' said Porter. 'Now do you recall where you were on

the fifteenth of July this year?'
'I was … I was at home.'
'All night?'
'Yeah.'
'Who were you at home with?'
'My brothers, my sister and my mother. And my dad.'
'Did you see any of your friends?'
'Nuh.'

Does he go out often with his friends? No, he doesn't. Where do they go? They catch a movie or play some pool, and go straight home.

'Alright,' Porter resumed. 'The allegation relates to the night of the fifteenth of July, a Saturday night.'
'Yep.'
'Now a lady went to the nightclub we drove you past today. And the allegation has been made that she was raped. That someone had sexual intercourse with her. Do you know what I mean by sexual intercourse?'
'No.'
'That a man put his penis in her vagina. And that she didn't agree to that. So it was against her will. Do you understand that?'
'Yeah.'
'She cannot recall this because she was unconscious. She thinks that something had been put in her drink to

affect her mind.'

'Okay.'

'Okay. I'm going to show you a photo of a lady. It's a licence photo.'

In this photo, which became a court document and was shown to the jury, Maria wears an intense expression. Hair tied back, her eyes peer out from behind thick frames. She is unsmiling; her mouth slightly open, lips slanting. Her gaze is brooding, anxious, slightly haunted.

'Have you ever seen this lady before?'

'Never in my whole life. Never.'

'Now this lady was found unconscious in the nightclub. And was taken to the Austin Hospital for treatment. She had some tests done that suggest that someone had sexual intercourse with her without her permission. Do you have any comment to make about that?'

'No. I … I've done nothing to this,' Jama's voice faltered, became even softer. 'I have … I haven't … I haven't … I don't know … I don't know.'

'Do you go to nightclubs? Have you ever been to a nightclub?'

'Nuh.'

'Okay. Have you been to a bar for a drink?'

'Nuh. I don't … I don't drink.'

'Ever?'

'Never ever. It's … it's against … it's against my religion. To drink.'

'What religion is that?'

'Muslim.'

'Have you ever had a drink—an alcoholic drink?'

'Never.'

'So you don't even know what it tastes like?'

'No.'

'What else does your religious belief say you can't do?'

'You're not … you're not allowed to have sex. Before marriage. Because we believe that sex is one of the biggest sin … except killing. See, killing is the biggest. And then sex is second. And drinking's third.'

'So you're a practising Muslim?'

'Exactly. I'm practising.'

'Do you … Do you go to church or…?'

'I go to mosque.'

'How often do you go to mosque?'

'I go there Fridays. And then some other t … some other times, you know, to go … go and pray. Because we pray five times a day.'

'I would like to take some fingerprints and a DNA sample from you. Do you know what DNA is?'

'Yeah. Sure.'

'And compare it with the DNA that's been taken from the

lady who's made the allegation. Then we can compare them and see if they're the same.'

'Do youse have the … what she says? I want to hear what she says.'

'She doesn't remember. She was found unconscious. She's had a medical examination, which suggests that she's had sexual intercourse with someone.'

'I'm … I'm virgin. I'm … I'm not allowed to do those things.'

Jama suddenly became animated. 'D… don't youse test that … if the … if the … if the guy or … if he's virgin or not?'

Porter said no, there's no way to prove a male is a virgin.

While clearly overwhelmed and confused, Jama nevertheless seemed possessed of a naive goodwill. Alas, Jama talked this time, and he almost certainly talked too much. I guess he assumed candour would save him. It should have saved him.

In the final moments of the recording played to the jury came sounds of crinkling plastic; ripping and rustling sounds. For a few minutes this is all that's heard. And then, 'Now Farah, what I need you to do with this is to place it in … on one side of your mouth and on the sponge, rub it against the inside of your cheek …'

Chapter 15

The jury listened to Jama's police interview on the fourth day of the trial: Thursday July 17, the day that threatened to descend into vaudeville. The running order struck me as significant; the interview was the lens through which jurors observed what came next.

A juror listening to the interview might have figured the Jamas rather unusual. The defendant didn't even own a bank account. Not a huge deal, admittedly, but in the spirit of Aussie independence these days even kindergarten kids are encouraged to have bank accounts.

And what of his claims to religious purity, such as his renouncing alcohol? Only a few days earlier Slim had asked Maria, 'I presume, *like most of us*, you've had the experience of being drunk on occasions?' Jama clearly wasn't 'like most of us'.

As for Jama's description of fornication as sinful, the jury couldn't know, wasn't permitted to know, he subscribed to the theologically dodgy but undeniably convenient Clintonian definition of sex, in which fellatio doesn't count. Jama's tragicomic offer to undergo a virginity test clearly didn't come across as the earnest gesture it was. The young man's grasp of biology was as limited as Detective Porter's expertise in cultural diversity.

⋈

The jury heard from the first Defence witness, Jama's father, Abdulkadir Jama Osman. Giving his evidence through an interpreter, the father said that on the evening of Saturday 15 July 2006, the night of the alleged rape, he was critically ill. Jama maintained a regular bedside vigil. The boy was checking on his father every twenty minutes and only briefly left the house around midnight to drive home a friend who had dropped by earlier. The father's story went something like this:

'I was very sick to the extent that I had to call all my children to say my last words. It was very serious. I was hit by a stray bullet [in 1991] and it is in my body. I was in my house in Somalia. The doctors told me they can't remove it. All this side is painful that … of … I have nervous problem … the nerve.

'Yes, Farah was with me. Him and the younger ones, and they were all reciting some recitations of the Koran to me. Mostly people recite to seeck (sic) people the Koran on sunset on Sunday so they started at sunset. It … it doesn't take long but I can recall them reciting some Koran. Farah is the most obedient person of my children, so he was with me all night.'

A tax invoice and attached receipt from My Chemist Northland Health and Beauty Shop dated the same Saturday were tendered to demonstrate both how the father was able to recall the date of these events, and that he was indeed ill on that day.

※

Forgive my perverse admiration for the prosecutor. He led the lambs so effortlessly to slaughter.

※

Even Slim's opening question carried an implicit accusation.
'Have you ever worked since you've been in Australia?'
'No, I'm sick,' the father replied.
'Is that because of the sickness you've described?'
'Yes.'
'And that's since 1991 that you've had this nerve problem?'
'Yes, it affects also the half part of my body, especially when it is cold.'
'Especially when it's cold. Why does it stop you from working?'
Slim was presumably casting doubt on the seriousness of the father's condition. The father's response came as a deserved slap on the cheek.
'In fact it was … at times I cannot … people will collect … I cannot control my urine …'
In what qualifies as the most excruciating exchange of the trial, Slim probed the man about when he had started thinking about what happened on that Saturday night in July. Perhaps it was only after Farah's arrest in November? Did he remember the morning the police came for Farah?

Yes, the father remembered. 'They came on morning time. Two police and one lady.'

The father tied himself in knots. At first he appeared to concede that it was indeed his son's police interview that had forced him to recall the Saturday night in July: 'July 15 is a special remembering day for me'. But as Slim pressed him, he said he couldn't remember when he first tried to remember the fifteenth because, well, he was very, very sick that day.

Again and again Slim attacked the father's credibility. No, the father couldn't recall if a doctor had visited.

'You were dying that day, weren't you?' Slim taunted. 'You were on your death bed?'

'That God has … God knows. I don't feel death.'

'But didn't you think that on that day you were maybe dying?'

'Yes, but if I am dying, God has prescribed my death that day.'

While doctors obviously still wrote him prescriptions, he had otherwise given up on them.

'I had opted for Koran recitation that day … I believe in God so I don't worry much.'

Was he worrying then? Or had he sincerely believed God would pull his family through this crisis? I also wondered if the father was just as hard to pin down in his own tongue. Or was the interpreter's English itself a work-in-progress? Was that the reason for the tortuous, convoluted phrasing, for all the talking at cross purposes?

I remembered reading, in one of the documents from my bulging Somali file, about difficulties that had arisen with

Somali interpreters. The quality varied significantly and clients often regarded them with suspicion, for reasons of clan rivalry or for other, more mysterious, reasons.

⬦⬦⬦

Among the medicines prescribed to the father was Tegretol, the same drug Maria used for her mood disorder. Soon after this fact came to light, a characteristically alert juror queried why the father took that drug. Slim milked the opportunity so serendipitously presented to him. He challenged the father with, 'I suggest Tegretol is not for pain.'

Crisp rose to justifiable combat; the jury was asked to leave the courtroom. It was unfair to use completely different evidence from an earlier witness to impeach the credit of this one, Crisp argued. For all anyone knew, Tegretol could treat a range of conditions. Judge Lacava pointed out that given the chemist receipt had been introduced by the Defence, he was inclined to let Slim probe the matter. So with the jury back, and the damage already done, the father explained that his doctor had prescribed the drug to treat 'my sickness on this part from tip to toe'.

Remembering what the Somali interpreter had said about the taboo surrounding mental illness, I comforted myself with the possibility the father was utterly oblivious of the thrust of the prosecutor's questions.

If you have a mental illness back home then God help you.

⬦⬦⬦

Slim asked the father if perhaps Jama had been 'confused'

when he initially told the police he didn't see any of his friends on the Saturday night.

'Maybe he was confused,' the father agreed. 'He has never had a problem like that before.'

'Like what?' Slim asked, sailing close to the sun.

'He has never had a problem like that before.'

Did he mean his son had never been questioned by police about an alleged sex crime before? Slim of course couldn't refer to the pool hall episode, but all the same had the father known about this earlier 'problem' with the police and simply made a foolish error in the witness box? Or was he completely in the dark about the pool hall episode because his 'obedient' son wanted to spare him the *shame*?

Unfathomable to most in the courtroom, not least to their own lawyer, the family elicited less sympathy and more suspicion at every turn. Crisp had initially foreshadowed a problem with the defendant's brother, Liban Jama, one of three alibi witnesses he intended to call.

'I've made some enquiries over time about his position,' Crisp told Judge Lacava, 'but I've been instructed that he's been receiving ongoing chemotherapy from Peter Mac and I have a letter from there, which I only received this morning.'

I felt a stab of pain: how much sorrow and strife could one family take? On top of everything else, a sick child. My gentle questioning of family friends about the brother's present condition came to nought. They had a vague notion the child had been ill, but said they were never told details.

By this stage the secrecy no longer shocked me.

Crisp appeared to be hinting at how hard it was for him to obtain frank and coherent 'instructions' from the Jamas, despite his enquiries 'over time'. Did the Jamas understand the importance of Liban's alibi evidence? Had they flinched at the prospect of parading their son's illness, or simply wished to spare him unnecessary trauma? I guess Crisp prevailed because Liban Jama appeared as a witness after all. Asked about his occupation, he replied 'student'. Crisp urged Liban to speak up, towards the back row. The barrister sounded as if he were directing a school assembly.

The best that can be said about Liban's evidence is that it didn't come across as rehearsed. He confirmed that he and Farah were home that Saturday night because his dad was really sick. He gave confused evidence about the arrival and subsequent movements of Farah's friend. He unhelpfully asserted that Farah never left the house 'not even for fifteen minutes … The whole night he was there, my brother'.

Time and again, Liban's narrative came unstuck. Perhaps Farah had informed him of the alibi provided to police? No, Liban insisted, Farah said 'not a word' about his alibi. And nor had Liban listened to a recording of his brother's police interview. He simply wasn't interested in listening to the recording. Actually, he couldn't remember whether Farah told him that he'd told police he was home all night.

As to his brother's weekly social schedule, most Saturdays Farah 'doesn't go outside'. He couldn't remember if Farah went out on Fridays. Farah didn't go out Friday nights: 'He plays games at home, so'. Yes, his father was gravely ill. No, he couldn't remember his father making a verbal will because 'he said so many words'.

'I can't remember if my father was sick on Friday,' Liban testified. 'I have a good memory that he was really sick on Saturday … I can't remember if my father was sick the next morning. Of course, I remember how my father was because he's my father! On Sunday he was sick, but not really as sick as that night, so.'

Crisp, Jama's counsel, tried to rehabilitate Liban. The short exchange between them made me cringe, though the jurors probably felt something else entirely. Yet more contradiction and prevarication, more meaningless squiggles in response to straight questions.

'Is there any reason why you said in this case you can't remember a number of things?'

'Because at the time I was taking some medicine like for my shoulder and that, because I had a collar bone way back.'

'Did that medicine affect your memory?'

'No.'

'Did that medicine have any affect on you two years ago?'

'It's got side effects but I can't remember the exact side effects, so.'

What shoulder and collar bone problem? What about the cancer and the chemotherapy? What had the father and brother known about the pool hall episode the night before? What role, if any, had Uncle Osman played in this tale of the dying father and the Koran?

Jama's friend, Abdulkadir Mohamed, was a student at La Trobe University. A photograph of him on the internet shows a man with fine cheekbones, a thin nose and eyes squinting with mirth. He was involved in the pool hall incident on the Friday. He also appeared as an alibi witness at the trial, despite having initially told police that on the Saturday night he did not go out or see any of his friends.

Once in the witness box, Mohamed explained his earlier statement about the Saturday night. He said he had 'probably' meant that he didn't 'go out, like, some other place, clubbing or something like that'. In evidence that would become significant for a host of reasons, Mohamed said he and Jama had, on a couple of occasions, visited nightclubs. He said that when Detective Porter first asked him about Saturday 15 July, he couldn't remember anything particular about that date. But after checking his diary he realised that La Trobe University had won a teaching award the day before, on Friday. And then he recalled that he had shared this news with Jama to convince his friend to join him at La Trobe the following year.

'I was just pushing him all day,' Mohamed explained, although whether the 'all day' referred to the Friday or the Saturday wasn't clear, 'and telling him about … and giving him, like, the evidence to show him like, you know, that La Trobe won an award! And, like, try to prove it to him that he should come to my uni.'

Crisp tendered Exhibit A3, a media release dated 14 July 2006 from La Trobe University entitled 'La Trobe University Wins National Teaching Awards'.

Of course, Mohamed assured the court, having arrived at Jama's house at sunset he, too, saw everyone congregating in the father's bedroom.

'I thought, you know, 'cause something like, bad, I thought happened to him or something, 'cause he was, like, on the bed and everybody's around him reading Koran at him.' Mohamed said he stayed in Farah's room all night, whereas Liban had earlier put him at the sick man's bedside.

Mohamed's evidence was perhaps most notable for what was not said but was constantly alluded to. He told the court that he and Jama and another friend had gone out to Edward's pool hall in Reservoir on the Friday. Nothing was said about what happened that night, of course, and the barristers seemed to swerve abruptly away from the subject. But the unmentionable pool hall incident strained Mohamed's story about the Saturday night, making it seem an elaborate concoction.

Did Mohamed honestly expect the jury to accept the cheesy scenario of two young men 'all day' discussing the pedagogical merits of various tertiary institutions? The irony is that surely for Jama and Mohamed the Saturday was memorable. It was, after all, the day after the night before; if Mohamed had indeed visited Jama that evening the two boys might have relished the opportunity to debrief. Unless, of course, engaging in some heavy sex play with a strange girl in the back seat of a car was so regular an occurrence it hardly rated a mention.

Chapter 16

On the fourth day of the trial, before Judge Lacava gave his charge to the jury, the inevitable happened. From the jury room came a question for the judge: why did the police have Jama's DNA on their database in the first place?

'We should have had money on this!' the judge quipped. 'The inevitable question has been asked.' To the jurors, the judge responded that this was 'irrelevant'. They were not to 'speculate' on it any further.

As would eventually become clear, a tragic paradox underpinned the trial of Farah Jama. To ensure he had a fair hearing, free of prejudice, the pool hall incident of the night before needed to be concealed from the jury; and yet concealing the incident, precluding any possibility of its airing in that courtroom, all but ensured his wrongful conviction. All the same, imagine what might have ensued had Judge Lacava given the jury a more expansive answer. Imagine if he had levelled with the jurors, told them Jama's DNA was on the police database because he had been investigated over a rape allegation that turned out to be false. Would jurors really accept the proposition that a young man was falsely accused of rape not once, but twice?

How often does lightning strike?

※

Judge Lacava's charge to the jury, his wide-ranging instruction on the law as it applied to the case, opened a can of worms, a fact immediately obvious to the barristers in his courtroom. What they did not know, however, was that the judge's faulty reasoning on one discrete, undoubtedly minor, aspect of the case would become critically important in Jama's bid for freedom more than a year later.

The problem centred on Jama's assertion to police that he'd never been to a nightclub.

During the latter part of the trial, Judge Lacava had begun to express concerns about Jama. He worried the jury might conclude that Jama had lied to police about going to nightclubs, and that the jury might take this 'the wrong way'. He worried they might infer Jama lied because he had a guilty conscience, in the same way they might infer that a suspect fled a crime scene because he knew he'd done wrong. He feared the jurors might conclude the youth's lie, to use the legal jargon, showed a 'consciousness of guilt'.

Only, the judge shouldn't have worried. There was no lie. He misunderstood the evidence. True, there had briefly been some confusion. Jama's friend, Mohamed, revealed that he and the accused had been to the nightclubs Chasers and Monsoon a couple of times. This cast doubt on Jama's denial. But Mohamed swiftly clarified that the two youths only started nightclubbing together from early 2007, once Jama had finished high school. Thus, when Jama told the police, back in November 2006, that he didn't go to nightclubs, he was telling the truth. Still, the judge remained fixated on nightclubs. The seed, planted by no one, sprouted into a sick, unwieldy growth. The judge decided he needed to warn the jury about the whole issue of lies.

So that afternoon, Judge Lacava told the jurors that according to law not every lie uttered by an accused could be read as proof of a guilty conscience. They had to be aware of this principle should they conclude Jama had lied to police about nightclubs. Not that Judge Lacava was suggesting they ought to conclude the youth had lied. Indeed, the evidence suggested he hadn't. And Judge Lacava sagely proceeded to highlight the very lack of evidence for the alleged lie that could be used by jurors to such devastating effect. Only, even then he botched it, screwing up the timeline of Jama and Mohamed's clubbing excursions.

The judge dwelt at painful length on an innocuous issue about which he ought to have kept mum, and despite his good intentions, probably made things even worse for Jama. The issue of the nightclub outings perhaps gave the jurors yet another reason to doubt Jama's glib characterisation of himself as an obedient Muslim resisting the temptations of a hedonistic society.

On Friday morning the jury heard the closing addresses of first Slim and then Crisp.

The prosecutor reassured the jury. He soothed and coaxed and comforted. As long they were satisfied the accused had penetrated Maria's vagina without her consent, they did not have to work out how she became unconscious or whether the rape took place in the toilet or somewhere else. They did not have to play amateur sleuths. The DNA evidence in this case, he said, was 'rock solid'. As for the alibi witnesses, they were the Jamas and a loyal friend. The jury might think the friend was roped in for the job. They might think the alibi evidence was on the whole 'a pretty artificial, synthetic contrived sort of account, cobbled together, not to be trusted'.

Crisp, Jama's counsel, had the harder job. Or was it the easier job? Crisp's contention was that no rape happened, full stop, or that if it did, Jama wasn't responsible. This last argument deployed essentially the same logic the police lab had used in the Jaidyn Leskie inquest: Jama was simply unlucky enough to have substantially the same DNA profile as a mystery male who had had sex with Maria.

Crisp contended it was highly unlikely that Maria had been raped in the club en route from the bar area to the toilets. He stressed there was no evidence about any man with dark skin at the venue; no evidence linking Jama with the nightclub or even the suburb of Doncaster. It was improper for the jury to ignore all other evidence and rely only on the DNA. And while sexual intercourse could occur without injury, this was after all an alleged rape and the jury may be troubled by the absence of any sign of physical trauma or complaints of discomfort from Maria.

He said the police forensic biologist, Deborah Scott, had

sounded like a 'stuck record'. There were many questions she couldn't answer. And, well, throughout the years, scientists have been proven wrong!

Jama had co-operated with police. He raised his alibi at the outset. He offered his DNA sample, offered his fingerprints and even offered to do a test to prove he was a virgin. What more could an innocent person do? And what more could the alibi witnesses do? After all, if anyone asked them, the members of the jury, what they had been doing on a certain date six months earlier, they too would have trouble remembering. It was 'easy sport' for the Prosecution to cross-examine these people. The Jamas and Mohamed were 'relatively simple people, people without guile of any sort'.

Simple people, people without guile of any sort? People who cobbled together an artificial, synthetic story, people you couldn't trust? Good Muslim boy or two-faced rapist? These were the competing narratives presented to the jury.

By now it could only really be one or the other. It couldn't be something in between.

On Friday, at the end of a long court week, Judge Lacava told the jury they should not feel pressured into a fast verdict. Court would reconvene on Monday. The court was adjourned. Maria probably cursed another weekend without 'closure'. Bail was granted. The Jamas took their boy home.

On Monday morning, the jury asked for Maria's evidence to be read out again. They retired to deliberate at 10.43 am.

Half an hour later they had reached a verdict.

In the dock, Jama stood up to meet his fate. At the word 'guilty', he would recall, his legs went numb and his body became so limp he nearly keeled over.

For years to come he would endure flashbacks of this moment.

Chapter 17

It was only after Judge Lacava had discharged the jury, thanking them for their diligence and forbearance, that the barristers launched into argument about what sentence Jama ought to receive, and that the pool hall incident got a proper airing. Jama's counsel tried to impress upon Judge Lacava his client's previously clean record. His client had no priors, Crisp said, no trouble with the police whatsoever save for one incident, the incident that led the police to obtain Jama's DNA in the first instance.

Crisp said his knowledge of the incident was scant because he didn't have any of the documents, though he had discussed the matter briefly with the Prosecution. Then Crisp gave Judge Lacava a mangled account of the episode. He placed the action at a pool hall in Preston, instead of in Reservoir, and on the 22 July, a week *after* the events in Doncaster. He corrected the date after Slim hastily pointed out his error from the bar table.

His client was at the pool hall, Crisp told the judge, with two 'associates'. They apparently went off in a car with a girl that they'd met there. The allegation was that sexual acts occurred in the car. When his client was interviewed by police he admitted taking part in some acts, which were not apparently vaginal penetration, and had claimed they were consensual.

The matter did not proceed as far as committal, Crisp said. Actually the charges did not proceed. Actually they weren't authorised by the Director of Public Prosecutions. Actually they weren't authorised by police. Crisp stumbled to the punch line, 'The matter did not proceed. However, that appears to be the explanation for the authorities having a DNA sample and that's how it found its way to the data base, if I am correct about all that.'

And Crisp was indeed correct about all that.

With four days of prison life behind him, Jama returned to the dock on Friday to be sentenced.

'The circumstances of your offending,' Judge Lacava told him, 'involved you introducing your penis into the vagina of a woman at Doncaster on 15 July 2006, without her consent.'

The judge told him his conduct was reprehensible, was a rape of the most serious kind. He told him the absence of any evidence that he had spiked Maria's drink or had planned the rape was more than outweighed by his repugnant opportunism.

'You raped her when she was in a most vulnerable state.

You obviously saw her and sized up the situation as she presented to you. Instead of assisting her and making sure of her safety, you raped her for your own immediate and short-lived sexual gratification.'

'The jury', said Judge Lacava, 'cannot have viewed the facts any other way'.

He told Jama the sentence had to reflect the community's disgust with this sort of crime as well as the victim's suffering. He had taken into account Jama's youth, his turbulent childhood and his otherwise clean record. He had also taken into account the fact that Jama probably wasn't responsible for Maria's bruising—the injuries most likely occurred when the security guards carried her from the toilets in an 'undignified' manner.

He told Jama that his complete absence of remorse meant he had little prospect of rehabilitation. Moreover, having seen Jama's father and brother give evidence—evidence that was rightly rejected by the jury—the judge was sceptical that close support from family would do much to assist his chances of turning over a new leaf.

He made Jama stand to receive his sentence. Six years with a minimum of four.

'Remove the prisoner.'

This leaves one last question about the proceedings.

Where, during those six days was Jama's mother, the woman who had followed her son to the police station and waited fearfully at reception? Where was she during the circus of alibi witnesses or while Crisp advocated Jama's good character or when the discussion ranged over the incident with the girl in the car the night before?

I learnt the answer from Crisp's remarks at the sentencing hearing. He told the judge of the boy's close, supportive family. He explained how during the trial Jama's father had to remain outside the court because he was a witness, and how his client's mother had also been there the whole time. Sitting outside the courtroom, the whole time.

Crisp elicited more on this theme from Osman, Jama's uncle. Jama's mother, Osman said in the witness box, 'was crying outside the whole day'.

'She says she will have to go to her home because we have seen her crying outside. It is not good for Australian population, and even African population, to cry outside and show that they are not happy for the court.'

Even with his nephew wrongly condemned, Osman professed concern for what the 'Australian population' might make of an African woman crying outside a courtroom.

Why had the mother declined the opportunity to affirm her son's innocence? Why had the woman, whom the Preston warehouse owner described to me as 'respectable', hidden her face from judge and jury? A close friend of the mother thought the most likely explanation for the woman's conduct was that speaking, or even showing her face in court, would simply have broken her.

'She could not face it, I think,' the friend said. 'She would have collapsed.'

The friend rejected my theory that the mother had chosen invisibility for cultural reasons. I had read reports about how some Somali women in the West continued to think it improper to express an opinion in a room of men. I also remembered the time I wanted to interview a middle-aged Somali woman for a newspaper article. Before the woman could speak to me she needed her husband's permission. As I speculated about the reasons for the mother's silence, something finally clicked about myself. A realisation as banal as it was depressing.

I recalled how during my outing with Jama on Lygon Street I had suggested that Islam played a role in his courtroom fate because, after all, his alibi witnesses claimed to have spent the Saturday night reciting the Koran and how Jama had conceded that was indeed 'kind of about Islam'. The more I thought about it, the more convinced I became that so much of what went on in that courtroom was, in a rough, shorthand sense, 'about Islam'.

The Jamas, I realised, felt compelled to respond to an accusation as *shameful* as rape, rape in a nightclub no less, with a strenuous assertion of piety and virtue. Perhaps they felt the only way to impress their authenticity upon the jury was to conform to a perceived stereotype of modest pious folk. They seemed oblivious to how poorly this caricature might translate in a Melbourne courtroom, but I thought I had some idea. I imagined in elaborate detail how the jury, the lawyers and the judge—each with their allotted rations of information, all of them enabled by the DNA evidence—had interpreted the rhetorical flourishes, the mysterious contradictions, the things unsaid. In the end, everyone arrived at the same view of the man in the dock.

In a sort of dreadful epiphany I suspected that had I been in that courtroom I may have been just as receptive to the idea of his guilt. I might have succumbed to a poisonous deduction in the same way I had leaned to the most damning interpretation of the mother's mute presence outside the court. *She said nothing*, I had been tempted to surmise, because *these men don't allow their women to speak. Perhaps they even believe a woman's testimony carries less weight than their own. They think that women ought to be silent and veiled and 'respectful'.*

Had I been at the trial, I might have speculated about whether the Jama men subscribed to the infamous view of that Sydney sheikh, who described immodestly dressed women as 'uncovered meat'. Perhaps, the toxic logic might have gone, these men secretly believe that women who go to nightclubs and drink alcohol, wearing tops with spaghetti straps and tight pants with no underwear, *are bad women asking for trouble.*

Chapter 18

In his interview with *The Age* journalist in August 2010, Jama related an unnerving episode that he said occurred at the Metropolitan Remand Centre, a maximum-security prison in the city's west, where I assumed he was incarcerated for the four days between the jury's verdict and the sentencing hearing. Noting a conviction for 'rape' on his paperwork, the prison guards called him a 'black bastard'. The taunt terrified him, as rapists, he well knew, were at the bottom of the pecking order. Even after Jama was cleared for transfer to the medium-security Loddon prison in Castlemaine, where he remained until the evidence that proved his innocence came to light, he concealed from other inmates the nature of his conviction. Throughout his incarceration, Jama lived in terror of being 'outed' as a rapist by prisoners who knew him from the Remand Centre.

In the few conversations I had with him, Jama invariably referred to his prison ordeal—'everything I went through *inside*'—though he was careful not to divulge any details. I was left with the strong impression he envisaged his book as a tell-all account of the indignities he suffered, which I never doubted were many and painful. Every time he mentioned his prison experiences, my discomfort spiked and I was forced, again, to grapple with the moral complexities of my task. I would be inevitably hijacking *his story*, commandeering this intensely personal chapter along with the others.

He was right, obviously. How could I ever know, ever really understand, what he went through inside?

I leafed through a series of incident reports, obtained through Freedom of Information with the names omitted, from Loddon for the relevant period.

I catalogued the fights between prisoners, the threatened assaults, the threatened suicides, the alarming and the petty. A prisoner threatened to stab his cell-mate, shouting 'I don't want to share with a smoker!' Another pounded a hole in the wall of the 'urine holding room', where samples for drug testing are stored. Another told staff he had swallowed a razor blade, but an X-Ray found nothing.

In June 2009 prisoner 'x', being in an agitated state, said 'the fucking [blank] get whatever they want!' He said, 'I am going to rally all the boys and bash these cunts!' I speculated, trying to fill in the blank. The fucking *blacks* get whatever they want? Was this what he had said? The fucking *Muslims*?

On a glorious winter's morning a few months after Jama and I had met, I went on a tour of Loddon gaol where Jama had endured sixteen months of torment. Actually, at various times during the tour I had to remind myself that Loddon, which opened in 1990, is in fact a gaol—one of the world's first open-plan, community-nurturing, fresh-air-worshipping gaols, but a gaol nevertheless.

A display cabinet at reception showcased numerous certificates and prizes and letters of praise from people who matter. I cast my eye over them as I waited for my tour guide. An undated award for 'multicultural excellence'; a plaudit for recognising minorities, particular categories of offenders and others with special needs; a certificate honouring Loddon as the 2001 winner of the 'pride in prisons' award for 'the beautification of internal gardens'.

The gardens were indeed the first thing I noticed once, security checks done, we walked through a door that had a sign reading, 'Don't slam me, I have feelings too', and ambled by the multi-faith chapel, en route to the pale brick, low-rise accommodation areas, named after the shire's rivers and creeks. Greenery cascaded over archways. Lovingly tended flower beds fringed impossibly trim lawns. Roses so vibrant they made my eyes water.

The Corrections Victoria website boasted of Loddon's 'range of accommodation options to suit individual needs', as if spruiking a retirement village. I saw them now. Four-bedroom self-catering units for low-security prisoners or those nearing release, a privilege bestowed by official decree, and not simply according to 'need'. I tried not to feast on private details as my friendly guide walked me through a unit. But as I glimpsed an overflowing ashtray on a coffee table and a handwritten list of positive affirmations on a bedroom wall, I felt a spasm of existential guilt. I had become the kind of person who could command a tour through the living quarters of people who, for faults of character or hard-luck twists of fate, could command very little, including basic privacy.

On his arrival at Loddon, Jama would have gone straight to the more traditional, more prison-like, Forest Block. Precisely how long he spent here, I can't know. A cell in Forest Block may have been home right up to his release. The block I saw had two levels of tightly packed cells, with a light-filled recreation area on the ground floor. The inside of one cell was as-seen-on-TV: a bunk, tiny shower and a toilet by the door. Peach-coloured doors, in harmony with the pastel colour code throughout, but metallic and heavy nonetheless. They would slam shut emphatically.

Jama would have heard that sound, the sound of being 'secured' in his cell, every weeknight at 9.10 pm, and at 7.10 pm on weekends. I do not understand why this ritual takes place at the ten minute mark, rather than at 9 or 7.15, just as I don't understand why on the weekends prisoners have less time for recreation rather than more.

At 7.50 am each morning Jama was 'let out' of his cell. After this, he would make his own breakfast in the kitchenette, and embark on the day's activities. I had read somewhere that he regularly worked out at the gym. I wondered if he also availed himself of the educational opportunities inside; whether he had pursued accredited training courses in Engineering or Construction or Transport and Logistics, or whether he had perhaps whiled the days away in one of the prison factories, welding or fabricating metal or packaging or screen printing. Had he been relieved to learn he would only be asked to undergo a sex offender program as his release date neared? Had he taken comfort from the array of food options when dinner swung round at 4 pm? Had he been appreciative of the 'Muslim meat pies'—as the prisoner-chefs in the industrial kitchen called them—on offer for lunch?

I could only imagine he lived for the Saturdays, Sundays or Mondays when his friends or family could turn up—only once a day, mind you—to the prison visitors' centre. Here they would be searched and then wait for him on plastic chairs, possibly snacking from a volunteer-run canteen, if open. From here they and Jama might have retired to a nearby meeting room for no more than two-and-a-half hours.

After this, Jama, one of sixteen inmates serving time for sex offences, would be returned to the company of the other 382 inmates. Of these, almost a year after Jama's trial, seventy-six were drug offenders, seventy-one had been convicted of offences against property and sixty-three were murderers. The rest were guilty of offences against 'good order', or robbery or extortion or were merely poor sods who had clocked up obscene amounts in traffic fines.

Because for all the talk about 'prison journeys', Jama surely never lost sight—nor should he, in the interests of justice, have lost sight—of the 7.5 metre-high wall that surrounded Loddon like firm hands around a neck. A pastel wall separated from the rest of the prison by a vacant and forbidding buffer zone carpeted by gravel and swept by sensors. Jama surely never lost sight of it, even as he looked out at the gently sloping coppery hills. Even when he took in this pretty Goldfields vista from the undoubtedly attractive open area near Forest Block, an area resembling a camping ground with basketball court and pool and barbecue table with faux grass roof, tropical style. And a line of totem poles, recognising (or even, 'celebrating'?—would people say that?) inmates from all corners of the globe; an eagle for North America, a lion for Africa and so on.

I doubt he would ever have lost sight of that wall and its meaning. Not as a new year ticked over, not as his birthday came and went; not as the local seniors were hosted for lunch, or as the Year 11 and 12 students visited for 'Loddon Awareness' workshops, or as a Feast of Eid, marking the end of Ramadan, was held in keeping with the prison's commitment to 'multicultural excellence'.

I doubt Jama even noticed the roses, let alone stopped to smell them.

Once the tour was over, my partner and I stopped briefly at the Old Castlemaine Gaol. Built in the 1850s, in response to escalating crime and disorder in the goldfields, the bleak Dickensian tower of metal bars and razor wire is, these days, a twee tourist attraction. I read on the tourist information board that the prison, based on the 'innovative Pentonville design', had exemplified the latest in penal system thinking. It was the Loddon of its time. On the way back to our car, I heard music from an office at the prison entrance that is home to a community radio station. The song was Billy Joel's *An Innocent Man*.

Chapter 19

With the trial having been reported in the media, the Jama family could no longer keep their son's predicament 'in the backyard', as one of their friends had put it to me. What had previously been the family's private trauma now became the community's collective burden. The Jamas were at last forced to set aside their pride and ask for help. And help came, even if many people harboured serious doubts about the boy's innocence.

Shortly after Jama's conviction, a delegation of Somali women visited his mother at the family home. They found her in an acute state, inconsolable with grief, but also vehement in her desire to clear her son's name. Every family friend I spoke with said the mother's passion, her sorrow and her determination lasted to the day of Jama's vindication.

'She was strong not to lose her mind,' one said, in a voice heavy with awe. 'She was crying day and night when he was in prison. Day and night.'

Just as she had wept outside the courtroom every day of her son's trial, so she cried every day of his incarceration.

I knew this woman well. On this score, I needed no 'cultural interpretation'. She was 'The Mother', her love frantic and raw and as blind as it should be.

⋈

When the women next visited Jama's mother she told them about a recent visit to her son in prison. She had looked him directly in the eye and asked him to tell her the truth. He returned her gaze and said, 'Mum, I didn't do it'. Of course he didn't do it! the mother told the women. Her son was no rapist. She knew that, and she would shift heaven and earth until the rest of the world knew it, too.

Still, the Jamas were up against it, and not just because of the forensic evidence that pointed to the boy's guilt. Money, or lack thereof, was a major problem. The other problem, understandably enough, was their lawyers, who, also understandably, refused to indulge the Jamas' claim that the DNA found in Maria was not their boy's. He didn't do the crime, the family argued, ergo the scientific finding had to be wrong.

A couple of weeks after Jama's conviction his original defence team filed an appeal. Presumably, they tried to convince the family that a narrow argument, largely about Judge Lacava's direction to the jury on nightclubs, was the only hope of setting aside the guilty verdict. I imagined they must have read the Jamas the riot act, in the way lawyers frequently do. I imagined they explained that a successful appeal would probably grant Jama a retrial, and then, well, one never knew, perhaps they could get lucky with a new jury, or perhaps new information might turn up to the boy's benefit. I imagine the lawyers also warned the Jamas that the chances of a different verdict second time round weren't good, and that the exercise, needless to say, would be costly.

Shortly after Jama's conviction, a delegation of Somali men went to see lawyer Michael Gleeson, Jama's solicitor at trial. Among the men in the delegation was Omar Farah, a rather enigmatic character with a trim moustache and husky voice, whose candour, I would go on to learn, could at times be disconcerting. A friend of the Jamas, he is also married to Zeinab, the community worker I had visited in Point Cook to discuss rape and other sensitive matters.

I met Omar Farah one morning in his office in Carlton, in Melbourne's inner city, from which he runs education and job training programs for men from the Horn of Africa. He told me he had only learnt of the boy's trouble through the papers. After the conviction, Jama's father approached him, along with a couple of others, for help. He remembered Jama's father and another friend of the family also attending the meeting at Gleeson's office in Melbourne's CBD. Omar Farah told me that he didn't like Gleeson's manner at that meeting. He recalled the lawyer enquiring about his name and position and connection with the Jamas. He seemed suspicious.

When I asked Gleeson for his response to this observation, the lawyer told me during a brief telephone chat that various people at that meeting were peddling unhelpful theories about the case, claiming, for instance, that the victim 'was in a conspiracy with the police. Those sorts of things,' Gleeson said. 'Things which were just ridiculous. And I didn't want to be discussing things with people who weren't entitled to be involved in the case and who were making frankly silly suggestions.'

In truth, Omar Farah himself had reservations about Jama's case. He couldn't accept the family's denial about the DNA evidence. He also had a niggling sense of people withholding information from him, which is, he sighed, the Somali way.

'Everybody goes as much mile as possible to protect their family from shame,'—again that word—'and that avoidance of shame puts them in a position where they deny the core of the issue. My problem was, I thought, "Well, for me to help you, you have to tell me everything".'

Still, at some point after the meeting he made a discreet enquiry about whether the Doncaster nightclub had an age policy and learnt that indeed only people twenty-eight or over could be admitted. So it was true, he thought. The place was officially off-limits to teenagers such as Jama; a strange business, for sure. But he took a back seat all the same. Relations between Somali communal leaders were strained at the time. There was tension between himself, his brother (a prominent figure, who has since become head of the Petroleum and Minerals Agency in Puntland, Somalia's relatively stable northeastern region) and Osman, Jama's uncle. Honest conversations were difficult.

He seemed to remember a community fundraising drive to enable the Jamas' new lawyer to pursue new investigations. Omar Farah thought he too made a donation to the fighting fund because 'culturally, I have to'. He sighed heavily again, his face gloomy.

'I believed the police, and I'm angry about that. I should have pressed … asked more questions,' he said. 'It really haunts me now.'

Even after his wrongful conviction, Jama's misfortunes in the legal system persisted—although he almost certainly contributed to his bad run by rashly hiring and firing solicitors.

Just weeks after his conviction, Jama dumped Michael Gleeson as his lawyer and made an overture to another solicitor, Theo Magazis. After a brief conference with Jama at the prison, Magazis agreed to act for the youth.

'I'm sure I wasn't the only solicitor he saw at that time, but that's quite normal, that's not a criticism,' Magazis told me during a brief phone conversation. He said he took no further steps, however, because the Jama family provided no funds. And no funds meant no work.

I understood what he was really telling me. The prisons are full of innocent men: Jama, for all he knew, was just like the rest. No sensible lawyer would run this one on faith alone—there was DNA evidence for goodness' sake.

But within three months of the conviction Kimani Boden, the handsome lawyer who was at Jama's side the day his innocence was proclaimed, had agreed to do just that, to run the prisoner's case almost on faith alone. So at the end of that month Boden asked Michael Gleeson for the file, only to be told the firm no longer acted for Jama and that Theo

Magazis was now handling the case. In the event, a deadline for filing a further document in Jama's appeal was missed and thus in the new year, six months after his conviction, the court automatically dismissed the appeal.

Jama would sit in gaol for another ten months.

Once the case was reinstated, the appeals prosecutor would read the transcript of the trial, learn of Judge Lacava's misconceived tangent about nightclubs and lies, and immediately grant Jama a retrial.

※

The Jamas settled on Kimani Boden because he appeared sympathetic to their cause. He agreed the evidence against Jama seemed flimsy and the circumstances strange. And his being African and Muslim made the family more inclined to trust him. The Brunswick lawyer had already earned a romantic reputation. Together with his wife and partner, Hina Pasha, in 2002 he fought a Supreme Court battle on behalf of small investors against a stockbroker represented by a top-end-of-town legal firm. They were victorious, winning their clients more than $1 million in damages. The media lapped it up. Here was David versus Goliath meets *The Castle*. A story in *The Age* focused on how the duo had waged this unequal war without even a photocopier in their office. Boden said his spiritual beliefs had helped sustain him through the battle.

The ABC's *Australian Story* explored the couple's history. 'It wasn't the first time that Kimani and Hina had the odds stacked against them,' went the introduction. 'Before they could make legal history, they had to win the battle to be together.' She came from a traditional Indian family with a belief in arranged marriages; he was part-African and had grown up in East Germany. For years they went to elaborate lengths to keep their relationship secret. But after Hina was injured in a serious car accident, Kimani would spend all night at her bedside, and his devotion finally won her family over.

Boden would tell the media that the first thing he did was ask the police for the file on the first complaint against Jama, the pool hall incident. The police refused to hand it over—it was an investigation only, and not a completed file. Boden then sought to have the original sample implicating Jama retested at a laboratory independent of the police.

When I learned the Jamas had also enlisted Sheik Isse Musse, a blind Somali cleric at Werribee, for help during their ordeal, I was quietly thrilled. It afforded the perfect opportunity to meet someone I had been observing with interest from afar. His responses to hot-button debates were often thought-provoking. After the arrest in 2009 of three Somalis for allegedly plotting to attack a Sydney army base, Sheik Isse strongly supported a ban on the Somali militant group, al-Shabaab, arguing it was long overdue. A year earlier he had called for polygamy to be legalised, citing the large number of single mothers in the Somali community who had legitimate emotional and financial needs but feared the stigma of sex outside marriage. And in a friendly gesture to Christians, he named his mosque, 'The Werribee Islamic Centre and Virgin Mary Mosque'.

So grand a title implies equally grand premises. Only driving back and forth along a flat road with nothing but suburbia and the odd empty paddock, I was confused. I had been expecting the Paris mosque—minaret, fountains, mosaic tiling—in Melbourne's west. The address itself revealed only a cluster of squat council-style houses, with driveways facing a paved communal space. Eventually I realised this had to be it, and soon enough saw the sign. I was greeted by the Sheik's wife, a cheerful raconteur with a radiant smile, who wore a pink patterned veil draped over a red-and-white checked dress. She showed me to a small meeting room with a table, a fridge and some shelves of religious texts.

A few moments later, Sheik Isse arrived, a thin man in loose garb leaning on a cane. His dark sunglasses lent an inevitable air of inscrutability.

He remembered ringing one of Jama's defence lawyers after the conviction to try and ascertain the facts for himself. While he couldn't remember the lawyer's name, he was left with the impression the man was certain of Jama's guilt and he wondered if a lawyer ought to at least feign belief in their client.

'I met the boy in prison. The family asked me to meet him because he was in shock,' the Sheik spoke with an infectious energy, gathering pace as he went. 'The family asked me to go and talk to him and console him and things like that. And I went. I went … and I thought the boy was lying, I thought, in the beginning, he was lying. And I sat with him and he was swearing, you know, and when a Somali man, a Somali boy, swears, you know "in the name of God, I did not do this, I did not do that …" In forty minutes he's repeating the same thing …' He raised his hands as if to say, 'What else could I do but believe him?'

'I said, "Well don't worry, don't worry". I advised him to keep his morale high, to become a bit religious, to pray, which some Somalis usually do when they go into prison.' He chuckled at the last bit.

We talked for a while, about the famine in his homeland, about integration. As we were winding up, I said I had heard that people in the community wanted him to deal with the growing sexual adventurousness of Somali youth. The young men were watching pornography, seemingly ignorant of Islamic moral codes. He spoke in the soothing voice one often hears from men of God. It was true, he said. Somalis are religious people, they want their children to behave a certain way. It is crucial that these children receive moral guidance. 'But still you can't control everyone. You cannot lock everyone up.'

Chapter 20

By the end of a criminal trial, the Prosecution file invariably takes on a worn appearance. The cream manilla folders heave from documents that have been steadily accumulated as a case moves from charges to verdict and beyond.

At the appellate stage, the file is stripped bare. Once Victoria's Office of Public Prosecutions is notified by the court registry that an appeal has been lodged, a law clerk opens a new file. The file, slim and blue, containing the appeal document and little else, is then handed to the Appeals Unit manager. It is a neat metaphor for the process by which Farah Jama was cleared, and the truth finally revealed. That process entailed a fresh set of eyes, an unsullied mind looking over the material. In this instance, the eyes—blue, assured and occasionally mischievous—belong to Brett Sonnet, a baby-faced appeals solicitor who received the file of *The Queen v Farah Abdulkadir Jama* two days after the appeal was lodged by Michael Gleeson on behalf of his convicted client. Sonnet's job was to oversee the Crown case against Jama's appeal.

At the time he received the file, Sonnet was a year away

from a ground-breaking promotion. In his early forties, Sonnet would become the first solicitor to be appointed an Associate Crown Prosecutor, and in the process shatter an assumption that 'Crownies' had to be picked from the ranks of experienced trial barristers. His achievement inspired both admiration and disquiet among colleagues. When I meet him in the OPP's main building in the city, he concedes he was 'perhaps not fully embraced by other Crownies', which perhaps meant that some fellow prosecutors were waiting for the chance to turn on him. As it happened, they didn't have to wait long.

Sonnet holds no grudges, though. Reservations about his appointment had some validity, at least in theory, and people were used to the way things were. He feels no rancour against these colleagues, just as he harbours no resentment against the careers counsellor at his alma mater, Chandler High School in Keysborough, where he ended up after his family moved from Gippsland to Melbourne. Everyone had expected Sonnet to become a labourer like his dad, not least Sonnet himself. Sweating it out alongside his father during the school holidays, he glimpsed his own future as a master builder. He saw it right up to the day an elderly neighbour was robbed and severely bashed in her home, at which point Sonnet, then in his second-last year of high school, decided he wanted to be a lawyer. Not a policeman, as others, baffled by his sudden mission to 'do the right thing by society', were suggesting, but a lawyer.

The careers counsellor advised Sonnet his goal was 'too ambitious', and he should aim for something more 'realistic'. Such 'realism' may have prevailed were it not for the newly-arrived migrant student, the Yugoslav girl, who landed at Chandler High the following year, nursing precisely the same dream and possessed of a ferocious will to see it through. The two of them teamed up, sweated over their books and became the first-ever graduates of Chandler High to gain admission to law school.

Honestly, Sonnet doesn't think badly of the careers counsellor, though he has kept a copy of the report that warned him against ambition. And he re-read the same report every so often in the intervening years during which time he graduated in the top twenty of his year at Monash University, won the prize for legal philosophy, knocked around the Prahran Magistrates' Court as a criminal lawyer, scored a job with Victorian Legal Aid and began, in 1998, floating his star at the OPP. (All the while coaching Olympic hopefuls at the Dandenong table-tennis club.) Even if he'll never throw out that report, he feels no rancour, you understand. The counsellor wasn't being malevolent. The school was just like that, the teachers just like that. It was just the way things were.

Sonnet skimmed the Jama file. He made a cursory investigation of the appeal grounds, such as they were—a notice of appeal being simply a holding position, with the argument still to be fleshed out. Jama's lawyers flagged they would argue, among other things, that the judge had erred in directing the jury about nightclubs and alleged lies and whether their client had exhibited signs of a guilty conscience.

Sonnet wasn't worried. After all, 'consciousness of guilt' evidence—an accused seen fleeing from the scene of the crime, that kind of thing—is usually devastatingly compelling.

And there were roughly five hundred criminal appeals clogging the system; about two hundred of them being appeals against conviction. And most of those convicted criminals were, needless to say, professing their innocence.

Sonnet delegated the file to another solicitor in his unit who would take care of the day-to-day running, subject to his supervision. For a long time little happened. The case crept along and then stalled. Three months after Jama's conviction, Sonnet received a letter from a new lawyer, Kimani Boden, advising his firm would be handling the youth's appeal. Then, early in the new year the appeal was dismissed for a missed deadline.

In late February 2009, Sonnet received another letter from Kimani Boden. In the letter Boden asserted his client's innocence. He said his client had the full support of his family and community. He asserted that the incriminating DNA sample had been contaminated at the police laboratory and demanded it be released and tested again. This signalled a change of tack from Jama's team. They no longer argued, as the original lawyers had at trial, that the DNA results had been wrongly interpreted. They now alleged contamination of the sample.

Sonnet's first instinct was to refuse the request. Imagine if the Crown were to routinely reward such gambits? The administration of justice would be crippled. Here, there had been for all intents and purposes a proper trial and nothing appeared untoward. Jama's lawyers had had their chance to request a re-testing long ago. These forensic samples were usually fragile and tiny, one poke too many could destroy it entirely. Then where would they be? What's more, by now Sonnet was aware this sample was the sum total of the Crown's case.

But it was precisely this fact, precisely because the Crown case rested on DNA alone, which made Sonnet a little uneasy. The absence of any other evidence was novel, no doubt about that. And there was the 'climate of the times' to consider. In the same month Jama had stood trial, a Victorian prisoner, Russell John Gesah was charged, amid much publicity, with the unsolved 1984 murders of a mother and child, Margaret and Seana Tapp. Barely a month later the charges were withdrawn when it was found the DNA evidence central to the prosecution's case had been contaminated in the police laboratory. The scientists had extracted DNA from a pair of jeans using a special solution which seeped into the blotting paper and from there onto the bench, contaminating the next sample. The DNA from the jeans was Gesah's from an unrelated offence. The next sample was clothing from the Tapp murder case. It was an embarrassing debacle for the police lab and forced a review of the DNA evidence in seven thousand cases.

Given the climate of the times, Sonnet decided it was prudent in this instance to go the extra mile. Perhaps if he acceded to the Jamas' request, however irregular, the Prosecution would be assured a clear run from there on. So in early March, Sonnet authorised the release of the sample from the police lab. A few weeks later he wrote a memo for the file confirming his decision and informed Boden he would consent to another test.

But again the case stalled. The case stalled even though Jama's appeal was reinstated in April, without opposition from the Crown. It would already be October once the sample was finally re-tested—a whole seven months after Sonnet gave it the go-ahead. For a whole seven months, the Prosecution, the Defence, the police and the independent labs wrangled over the conditions under which the re-testing, which also necessitated a fresh cheek swab from Jama, would take place. The problem was that the Defence had demanded things be done their way.

'The Defence told us two things, acting on instructions,' Sonnet said. 'That the re-testing was not to take place in Victoria and that no female was permitted to be involved in the entire process.'

My jaw dropped. We were in Sonnet's office in Lonsdale Street. He was sacrificing the afternoon to give me a thorough account of the final chapter of the Farah Jama case. Sonnet paused for a moment and nodded with raised eyebrows.

'They said what?'

'They said Jama would refuse to co-operate with the provision of a DNA sample if a female was involved. That's what they said: "no women".'

No women. By that, they didn't simply mean the investigating police officer, Karen Porter, who would ordinarily be expected to supervise the taking of a new cheek swab from Jama, accompany the sample on its journey and liaise with the police forensic biologist. They actually meant no women, full stop.

But should the revelation really have come as such a surprise? I already knew Jama wasn't bashful about declaring the excessive power of women in Australian society. Did the Jamas believe females to be essentially incompetent, incapable of executing so delicate an operation without fouling things up? Or did they also perceive women as impure or unclean, their very presence likely to contaminate all over again? Or was this a more complicated prejudice, which overlapped with the idea of women as impure, and stemmed from an opinion, whether newly formed or longstanding I simply couldn't know, that females in what Jama had referred to as 'this society' were intrinsically malevolent?

Yet, seen from the point of view of Jama and his family wasn't there a twisted logic to it all? I could almost forgive them for suggesting, as they had done in the meeting with Gleeson, Jama's original solicitor, that the youth was a victim of a feminist conspiracy, for themselves joining the dots and coming up with a sinister picture.

First a woman engages in oral sex in a car, only to cry rape afterwards. Then another woman goes to a nightclub wearing a singlet top and no underwear, consumes several drinks in a short space of time, passes out and then, after a female doctor does some tests, Jama gets accused of rape, again.

Then a female police officer comes to arrest him for the rape of a woman he doesn't even know at a nightclub he's never even been to. Then to top it all off, a female scientist gives evidence at his trial that yes, the DNA found in the nightclub woman is almost certainly his when it couldn't be, it just couldn't be; he didn't even know her, he wasn't even there.

***

The second time I visited Brett Sonnet, on a spring morning in 2011, he wore dark pants, a grey T-shirt with a black swirling design, black socks and no shoes. His eyes looked puffy with fatigue, his face unshaven, his stubble speckled with grey. Were he not bald, his hair would have been ruffled. I asked if he had slept all night in his office.

'Almost,' he said. There was a case pending, I would be reading about it soon, he confided.

It was a murder case involving warring Lebanese crime families and it was doing his head in. An accused had confessed and then reneged, saying that a crime boss with a string of violent 'priors' did it, saying the guy shot the victim in the back repeatedly and had forced him to take the rap. The problem was the evidence wasn't definitive either way. Either of them could have done it. It had to be one of them, but which one?

He grabbed a paper and pen and drew a diagram of the crime scene: the victim, the car, the possible trajectories of the bullets. He took me through the alternative scenarios, the strength and weakness of each, feverish with excitement. For about twenty minutes I listened, intrigued, still standing up as I had walked in, bag on my shoulder. I noticed on his shelf an open loaf of Multigrain, box of margarine, also open, a packet of ham slices and a plastic bag with a tomato inside. Grinning, I gestured at the DIY sandwich bar. 'I'm trying to lose weight,' he said, patting his belly. I tried to explain that what I found amusing was his having brought all the ingredients to the office, rather than spend three minutes making a sandwich at home. It suggested a person utterly absorbed in work, impatient with the prosaic demands of daily life.

The Defence also wanted an independent person to witness the transfer of the sample from the police lab to another laboratory. For a time they demanded that the laboratory be in Tasmania, '… and as you can imagine,' Sonnet scoffed, 'the logistics of that would be extraordinary'. The parties argued about the cost, about the risk of a break in continuity during transportation of the sample—which would leave the Prosecution unable to verify its integrity, and almost guarantee Jama a re-trial and viable defence—and about the risks of contamination in so elaborate an arrangement.

By the end, Sonnet had had a gutful. He wasn't going to cop all the conditions, the ban on females included. The re-testing would be done his way or no way. After all, he was the one granting a most unusual indulgence.

Finally, the parties agreed to send the sample to Genetic Technologies, an independent, reputable and properly accredited lab in inner-city Melbourne. The laboratory received a portion of the DNA extracted from the original sample—the cervical swab itself having been used up in the original analysis—and a new cheek swab was taken from Jama in prison.

By mid-October the results of the re-testing were in.

Negative. That was the bottom line of a long, complicated report that landed on Sonnet's desk, bowling him over. Negative for any DNA profile. No DNA matching that of Farah Jama was detected.

How could this be? The case that had been little more than a mild irritation for Sonnet began to command his attention. The following week he and a junior colleague attended a meeting at the police lab at Macleod. They arrived early afternoon and would emerge three hours later.

Sonnet opened proceedings with a short speech to all assembled, a group that included Deborah Scott, the scientist who had testified extensively at Jama's trial.

'Okay,' he began. 'I'm the dumbest person you ever met, but there's a problem in this case because if you accept what Genetic Labs say, then there's no DNA match. So I want you to explain everything to me. I want you to explain how this is possible.'

In the hours that followed Sonnet asked question after question. He learned how the police came to hold Jama's DNA in the first place and how this earlier and unrelated incident had taken place the night before Maria was found unconscious in Doncaster. He asked the same question Detective Karen Porter had asked nearly three years earlier: might one sample have contaminated the other in the police lab? Again, the scientists assured him it wasn't possible. Much time had elapsed between the testing of the two samples, during which hundreds of cases were dealt with, the benches wiped down and sanitised each time. Different people had examined each of the samples at different times, on different benches and using different processes.

Sonnet agreed it was extremely unlikely the sample could have been contaminated at the police lab.

He then asked about the original test results. The more he studied them, the more troubled he grew. Certain things didn't quite stack up. For instance, did anyone think it odd that the amount of sperm detected on the one slide was so minuscule? Only one intact sperm and little more than a dozen fragments, when an average ejaculate contains tens of millions? Did anyone think that strange? Not really, the scientists replied. After all, the details of the rape weren't known. No one could say for how long, or even how, Jama had penetrated Maria. And without this information you simply couldn't see the amount of sperm as a sign of anything being awry.

Sonnet conceded the point. He looked at the test results of the two vaginal swabs and the two cervical ones. Wasn't the negative result from the 'vaginals', the absence of any sperm on those swabs, a problem? Not really, they said. They'd seen such a scenario before. The vagina is a hostile environment for sperm. Only the fastest and toughest reach the cervix.

Sonnet continued to press them. What about the sperm showing up on one of the cervical slides, but not the other? Two swabs taken from the same place, but only one comes back positive? Now wasn't that rather odd? Well, yes, that was rather unusual, the scientists agreed. Not impossible. But admittedly rather unusual.

'So then I said to them, "Okay, now what about the discrepancy between the lab's results and the results from Genetic Technologies? How can you explain that?" The scientists floated a number of explanations. Given the small size of the sample, perhaps Genetics' processes or instruments simply weren't sophisticated enough to detect the DNA. Or perhaps the DNA wasn't scooped up once the instrument was inserted into the test tube. The DNA had a tendency to cling to the side of the test tube, they explained. Perhaps if someone had shaken the test tube and swept the instrument along its side, the material would have been picked up.

'So I said to them, "Look, I'm still sceptical and I'm still dumb so here's what we're going to do".'

He wanted them to re-test and verify the results from other forensic cases that had been examined around the same time as this sample. He wanted the lab to again investigate the possibility of contamination from any other sample containing Jama's DNA. Lastly, he wanted the remaining DNA sample re-tested yet again, even though this meant it would now be entirely consumed. He insisted that no scientist or technician involved in the original test could take part in the re-testing; in other words, no one with a personal stake in the test results was to be allowed anywhere near the sample.

The police scientists were accommodating. After all, their reputation was on the line.

So they worked with speedy precision, reporting back to Sonnet before the month was through.

Yet again the scientists categorically ruled out the possibility of contamination from the earlier sample containing Jama's DNA. They verified original results from more than two hundred cases that had been recorded and examined at the same time as Maria's swabs. As for the sample in question, it was re-tested on 27 October exactly as Sonnet had decreed. The result: positive. The original outcome was confirmed. The sample indeed contained DNA matching that of Farah Jama.

Two results for, one against. Two positive for DNA matching that of Farah Jama, one negative. Now what was Sonnet supposed to do?

Once Boden was informed of the test result from Genetic Technologies, he applied for Jama to be released on bail pending the appeal. For Jama to be granted bail, he would have to point to a reasonable prospect of winning his appeal. This meant that before Sonnet could prepare a bail submission he had to know everything about the case. So for the first time, Sonnet called for the transcript of the five-day trial of the *Queen v Farah Jama*.

By the time he was done reading, he was sure of two things. Firstly, that the Crown was sunk on Jama's alleged 'consciousness of guilt'. It was nonsense, basically. The youth hadn't lied about going to nightclubs, and there was simply no basis for Judge Lacava's lengthy direction on the subject. Jama would almost certainly be granted a re-trial on this ground alone. It was pointless for the Prosecution to even put up a fight. Sonnet was also sure of something else, something so huge it eclipsed all the other considerations. Admittedly, he had reason to read the transcript with a degree of scepticism. Still, he wasn't expecting this—shadows and smoke, shrouding an implausible, empty core. The guy simply couldn't have done it. The case was a bizarre fiasco.

It began to gnaw at him, at first an inkling, then an obsession: Farah Jama was truly innocent. Sonnet decided then that he didn't want to grant Jama a re-trial. He wanted to deliver him an acquittal.

And, as both an officer of the Crown and an officer of the court, it was Sonnet's duty to ensure the Prosecution exercised its powers with the utmost integrity, to honour the truth above all else. Prosecuting counsel were 'ministers of justice,' expounded the Supreme Court in a notable judgment more than thirty years earlier, 'who ought not to struggle for a conviction nor be betrayed by feelings of professional rivalry' but 'make certain that justice is done as between the subject and the State'.

Sonnet took this job description very much to heart. If a grave error had occurred, he had to rectify the wrong as a matter of urgency. This much at least was crystal clear.

But how would he prove the youth didn't do it?

His subconscious was beginning to stir, but in truth he had no bloody idea.

What Sonnet did know was that the Prosecution had no grounds for refusing the request for bail. He spoke to his senior colleague, the 'Chief Crownie', Gavin Silbert SC. Sonnet told him they would definitely go down on the 'consciousness of guilt' question, which meant a re-trial was inevitable, and as Jama had been allowed bail before the original trial, there was no reason to oppose it now. He then needed to inform the victim and a number of others that Jama would soon be out on bail. Sonnet swallowed hard and arranged a meeting. The meeting lasted about an hour. Maria was there. She appeared an ordinary, well-dressed, middle-aged woman. Detective Karen Porter came too, as did her supervisor, whose presence Sonnet thought pretty unusual. The case was obviously a bigger deal for the police than he had guessed. (My approaches to Porter were re-buffed: 'Not this case', she apparently said—she wouldn't be saying a word about this case.)

The Crown simply had to agree to bail, Sonnet began. He took a deep breath and continued. But the Prosecution's problem ran much deeper: the Prosecution would struggle to prove Jama was guilty beyond reasonable doubt. His audience recoiled in shock. And then anger. No way, they said. He, Sonnet, was wrong. How could he think that? There was still DNA—okay, one negative reading alongside the two positives, but surely it was enough! Well, Sonnet said, after reading the transcript he no longer thought it was enough. In fact, he had come to the firm belief that the case amounted to 'a substantial miscarriage of justice'. One of the detectives said they would demand another prosecutor handle the case. 'Well, we'll see about that,' Sonnet said.

As for Maria, even as her world was being tilted upside-down, she was respectful and dignified. At least that's how Sonnet remembers her. It's how everyone from this time remembers her.

So at the bail hearing on 18 November 2009, the Prosecution kept mum. Boden informed the court that Jama, if released, would live with his parents and had the opportunity to work at the Flemington restaurant which, he said, was operated by Jama's mother. The family, he argued, also needed Jama at home as his eldest brother was recovering from an operation 'on his collar bone' and required a full-time carer.

Bail was granted. The Jamas, for the first time in sixteen tormenting months, would be taking their son home.

December neared, the season of festivities already kicking off. Amid talk of summer holidays and long lunches and Christmas parties, the Office of Public Prosecutions was preparing to wind down. But Sonnet was in an entirely different frame of mind. The Jama case had begun to throw him off balance, all but consuming him.

The fact that the young man was convicted without a shred of evidence to place him at the nightclub—no eyewitnesses or security footage, no phone or car records—was one thing. Quite another was the sheer absurdity of the proposition that Jama executed the rape, with lightning efficiency, in under half an hour.

To believe the Prosecution's case was to believe Jama to be a predator of extraordinary stealth and cunning. This wasn't the kind of rape scenario that police and prosecutors commonly confronted: boy meets girl, followed by a fraught encounter, followed by he said, she said. This was the case of a man who slipped unseen into a nightclub, chatted up his victim, spiked her drink, dragged her to the women's toilets, pulled up her pants after he was done violating her, jumped over the locked cubicle and managed to flee the crime scene without catching the eye of a single witness. So cunning was this man, he pulled up the woman's pants in the hope she might not even realise what had been done to her. So calculating, he even left the door locked, daring instead to scale the wall, to ensure his victim not be found straight away. By any measure, a breath-taking performance. An utterly improbable performance.

But then why was Jama's DNA present? How to explain that? It was a brain teaser, a special kind of torture. For three nights in a row he couldn't sleep. He lay awake, he paced around. He scanned his bookshelf for inspiration …

'If you were to come to my house you would see I've got just about every Agatha Christie novel in print,' Sonnet explained. '*Death on the Nile, Murder on the Orient Express* … I've read them each about ten times.'

Giddy with insomnia, he wondered what Miss Marple,

the doddering old spinster from St Mary Mead would do. How would the obsessive Belgian detective Hercule Poirot, who brought order and system and method to bear on every case, unravel the mystery of Farah Jama? Then one night, it was most likely a Wednesday or a Thursday, Sonnet woke suddenly at 2.30 am and thought, 'I know how he's not guilty.' In a thunderbolt the answer hit him—14 July, *the night before.*

'How does Miss Marple solve crimes? She looks at the psychological profiles of people. And she works out from that who would have committed the crime. So that's why I wanted to look at the material about the night before—I wanted to look at who Jama was. Who is Jama? Is Jama this predatory rapist? Because that's what we're saying he is. And if he is, then the night before we ought to see some evidence of his predatory character.

'If this man is guilty he would have performed in an identical manner the night before because human beings are creatures of habit. And I knew that the night before he was alleged to have sexually abused a young woman. If he was truly guilty, he would have used a similar *modus operandi*. Gone to a disco, slipped drugs, pulled up her pants.'

It had to be all about the M.O. Sonnet was now convinced the answer would be found in Jama's first police file, the file of the pool hall incident in Reservoir.

⋈

The only possible exception to the psychological rule of thumb about people being creatures of habit, Sonnet ruminated, was illness or some other such thing. People suffering certain conditions do act erratically. So after Sonnet arrived at the office the following morning, after he urgently called for the first police file, he enquired about Jama's health.

Did the boy have a mental illness? Had he suffered a brain injury or anything like that? No, came the reply. Jama was a normal teenager. He finished high school, there was nothing unusual about him in that sense.

Sonnet was satisfied. With a rush of anticipation, he opened the file and started reading.

Chapter 21

At the other end of the line, Ella spoke in mild 'strine'. She was happy, and rather intrigued, to talk to me, especially after she learned I wouldn't, indeed couldn't, print her real name. Of course, the events of Friday 14 July 2006 happened so long ago and her role in the drama was very minor. But, sure, she'd gladly tell me all she remembered.

At the time, Ella was living with her baby in Reservoir, having moved to Melbourne from country Victoria. Her old high school friend Taylah, who, like her, was nineteen and a single mother, had left her toddler in the care of his grandma and come to stay for the weekend.

In the evening, she, Taylah and some other friends had a few drinks at home. Probably Jim Beam, because that's mostly what they drank. Drugs? No, no drugs. She can't stand drugs. She won't allow drugs in the house. Neither does she like getting drunk before going out because 'that's when things always happen'. She's one of those 'cautious types'. So that night they drank 'a little bit, nothing spectacular, maybe one or two glasses' and then wandered round the corner to check out the pool hall, Edward's Place.

'Anyway, we went in there. Tay said she was going to have a look around. Me and my mates were sitting at a table. And after a bit we wanted to go home, and Tay was sitting on a couch talking to this one guy and she said she wanted to stay. And me being a rude person I said, "Well, if something happens, don't blame me". I don't really like leaving my friends behind. I know, I was a bit of a bitch, but, you know, I've been raped before; when I was sixteen I was raped … on the way to school and'—I flinched at the casual, throwaway delivery—'back then, Tay was a bit too trusting of people in general. I'm not saying that's a bad quality … but … when you're meeting people and you're up and about …

'Anyway, we were back home watching TV when Tay suddenly rushed in. It was late. I can't say exactly how late, but very late. And, you know, Tay was meticulous about how she looked all the time. But her make-up was running, her hair was messed up. She ran into my bedroom, plonked herself on the bed. She was crying. She said she had been forced to do stuff. I can't really remember, but it was something along the lines of 'heads and blow jobs'. Three guys. It was in the back seat of the car. They took her somewhere local. So me being me I freaked out and called the coppers.'

The 'coppers', from Reservoir police station, from the Criminal Investigation Unit and the Sexual Offences and Child Abuse Unit, arrived promptly on Ella's doorstep. Officers took Taylah for a rape medical examination; Ella tagged along for moral support. They took a detour through the surrounding streets so Taylah could identify the alleged crime scene, the secluded spot to which the men had driven her hours earlier. She found her bearings, and established for police that the men had driven her to the Lakeview Tennis Club on Leamington Street, a quiet strip near a parkland estate that encompasses Edwardes Lake.

At Taylah's medical, the doctor bagged her clothes for forensic analysis. In her highly agitated state, Taylah gave a rambling account of where the guys touched her and what they did. By now it was nearly 4 am on Saturday morning. The doctor, according to a statement, took four oral swabs and corresponding slides for sperm, a skin swab of Taylah's right breast for 'foreign DNA', including saliva, 'and a vaginal swab and an anal swab … for foreign DNA, in view of the allegations of digital penetration'. A portion of Taylah's hair that was matted with semen was also cut and placed into a yellow screw-top plastic specimen container.

In the evening Taylah made a formal police statement. She told of meeting a 'black' man and his two male friends at a billiard hall in Reservoir. The man asked her if she wanted to go for a drive. She agreed. Taylah, the man and two of the man's friends climbed into the car. They drove a short distance to the tennis courts on Leamington Street. Taylah alleged she was then forced to perform oral sex on all three men. She claimed that she had tried unsuccessfully to pull her head away from their penises during the encounter. That she had said to one of the men, 'Stop, I don't want to do this,' to no avail. That she even tried to resist by using her teeth on one of the men: 'I gave him, like, a hard nip and he said "Ow".'

Over the next few days, the police investigated Taylah's complaint, now codenamed 'Operation MUTUEL'. They visited Edward's pool hall and obtained from the proprietor the video surveillance tape for the night in question—in vain, as it happened, because the tape was found not to contain footage. But with Taylah's assistance the Criminal Identification Squad had a description of the car and a computer reconstruction of the face of at least one of the men, and before long they were able to identify the suspects as Farah Jama, Abdulkadir Mohamed and Abdulkadir Abdullah.

About a week after the incident, police interviewed Jama. He admitted to the encounter, admitted he had ejaculated into the woman's hair, but said the acts were entirely consensual. The other two men independently gave police the same account. Nevertheless, Jama and one of the other men agreed to a routine request to provide police with a DNA sample.

When the police, ten days after the incident, confronted Taylah with the men's version of events, she conceded most of it was true and essentially recanted her story. In a revised statement, she admitted to having made a number of arguably suggestive remarks in the car. She had confided in the men about her recent involvement in a 'foursome' and had remarked, 'Once you've had black, you never go back'. She'd also told the men her friends had wagered she wouldn't last six weeks without sex. And she confirmed to police a critical omission from her earlier statement: at one point during the encounter in the car she had yelled out, 'Fuck me! Fuck me!' Taylah concluded the three guys may have misunderstood her, '… and thought that I was consenting to the sexual acts because I didn't really resist'. She agreed they were all 'just going with the flow'. She requested the police take no further action. While the police could still have charged the men, even against the woman's wishes, the head of the Sexual Crimes Squad, acting on the recommendation of his detective colleague, decided not to do so. The detective had concluded that on any reading of the evidence the woman was consenting 'to some if not all of the sexual acts that took place'.

Taylah may have withdrawn her complaint, but her forensic samples, including the lock of semen-crusted hair the doctor had snipped and bagged only hours after the pool hall incident, proceeded on an orderly journey through the police lab. Even though Taylah's case did not proceed, even though Jama would never be charged, police were nevertheless entitled to hold on to a suspect's DNA for an entire year before it had to be destroyed. Once received by the forensics lab, the samples containing Jama's DNA were routinely tested and stored in accordance with this law.

Thus, the week after the pool hall incident, police forensic biologist Deborah Scott, the same scientist who had charge of Maria's samples, a connection that's curious though almost certainly incidental, took Taylah's samples out of storage for testing. By mid-August the DNA profile of Farah Jama, extracted from both the semen found in Taylah's hair and from the cheek swab he had agreed to give police during their investigation of her complaint, was placed on the forensic database.

And the rest, we know. About a fortnight later, on 8 September, the DNA profile recovered from Maria's cervical swabs landed on the database, and came up a perfect match to Farah Jama.

To Brett Sonnet, the police file was the Book of Revelation. Finally, he had his answer. As he had suspected, Jama's conduct, whatever one might say about it, was not that of a calculating predator. He was in the back seat of the car with a fully conscious and apparently game young woman who even demanded to be 'fucked'. He gave police a full and frank account of events. He consented to a DNA sample. Many teenagers get involved in this kind of stuff every other weekend.

In short, his M.O. (*modus operandi*) supported his innocence. What young bloke declines an offer of vaginal sex from a woman his own age on one night, and barely twenty-four hours later, in another part of town, drugs and vaginally rapes a woman thirty years his senior? He reckoned it contradicted the basic laws of human nature, was far-fetched to the point of absurd. Of course, this still didn't explain why Jama's DNA was found on Maria's swab. But as I said, Sonnet had his answer. It was contained in the report of Taylah's medical examination on the night of the incident. Taylah was taken to the Austin Hospital. She was examined in the room maintained by the Centres Against Sexual Assault. Her forensic medical officer, the doctor who had cut her matted hair, was Nicola Cunningham. Same hospital, same bed, same doctor and just twenty-eight hours between the examinations.

Sonnet grinned. A thought popped like a champagne cork.

Bingo.

Sonnet called Deborah Scott from the police lab. He explained he had discovered the two women were examined by the same doctor in the same room and only a day apart. Could the sperm from Taylah's hair have somehow contaminated Maria's swab? Scott said indeed it could have. Dried semen sheds fragments of DNA all the time; it carries a high risk of contamination, the highest in fact. Bits of semen could easily have fallen on to the surrounding surfaces, for instance.

Sonnet collected his thoughts and wrote a twenty-page memo to the Chief Crown Prosecutor, Gavin Silbert SC, laying it all out. He concluded that all the evidence pointed to Jama having suffered a serious miscarriage of justice.

'Whilst it is not necessary to go any further,' he wrote, '*I am inclined to the view that Jama is truly innocent of any wrongdoing.*' Two days later Silbert, having read the memo, was unequivocal.

'He's an innocent man,' he said to Sonnet.

That Friday afternoon Sonnet approached the Director of Public Prosecutions, Jeremy Rapke QC, with a copy of the memo in hand. He explained the circumstances to Rapke. The Director didn't need to read the memo. What he heard was enough to make the call. Rapke gave one order—get this man off, and fast.

Sonnet contacted the Victorian Institute of Forensic Medicine, Cunningham's employer, and told them about the likelihood of contamination in a case that years ago resulted in the conviction of a young man. After an investigation at their end, the Institute's director, Professor Stephen Cordner, swore an affidavit conceding it was possible that processes the Institute relied upon, 'may have resulted in the contamination of swabs taken during the examination of the alleged victim of this case'.

Maria was no longer a victim but an 'alleged victim'. Within a few days, Sonnet would go further still and tell the Court of Appeal it was possible Maria hadn't been raped at all. Even then he was being rather circumspect. It was a dead certainty nothing happened to Maria on Saturday 15 July 2006 at Venue 28. Nothing other than her drinking too much while on medication, zoning out as she staggered to the toilet, undoing her button and zip for the usual reason and then losing consciousness.

At the Institute's Southbank headquarters the staff were reeling. The head of clinical forensic medicine, Associate Professor David Wells, first heard of the crisis from a shaken

Cunningham. Once all the circumstances became clear, Cunningham's mortification was complete. She already knew this would become one of the most bruising episodes of her career. The Institute chiefs, Wells included, would spend the next few months telling anyone who'd listen (from retired Supreme Court judge Frank Vincent QC, who would lead an inquiry into the case, to the media), that had the police laboratory passed on Detective Porter's query about contamination, had the Institute been informed of any concerns with the samples, they would have immediately traced the samples back to their source. They would have twigged to the connection between Taylah and Maria, and that knowledge alone would have set off alarm bells impossible to ignore. As it was, they knew nothing—once the samples are handed to the police, the Institute's work is done.

And Wells, a lean and urbane man in his fifties, would also tell anyone who'd listen that it was entirely unfair and undeserved for Cunningham to take the rap. According to Sonnet's people-are-creatures-of-habit theory, the doctor was the vital link in the chain of mishaps. She would, for instance, have placed the swab or the scissors down on the same spot the next night as she had the first, when, among other things, she snipped a piece of hair crusted with semen. But the theory is nonsense, Wells insisted. The outcome would probably have been no different had another doctor examined Maria. It was a constant source of frustration for the Institute that it had no control over these rape crisis units, including the nine that are physically attached to public hospitals.

The advocacy group, the Centres Against Sexual Assault,

ran them, whereas the hospitals were technically charged with cleaning the individual rooms. The Austin was supposed to have thrown out the disposable items on the trolley and restocked it. But it was unusual for two suspected rape victims to turn up over the same weekend, and in the often stretched Emergency Department, hospital staff had more pressing issues to deal with than cleaning a rarely-used examination room. Almost certainly no hospital cleaner would have thought to decontaminate the moveable light above the bed, or the trolley's top or the items left on its surface.

Wells was emphatic. It simply wasn't Cunningham's fault. The whole arrangement was a disaster waiting to happen—he knew of one hospital where the orderlies threw impromptu parties in the crisis care unit, ordering in pizza and everything!

And he would tell anyone who'd listen, 'Nicola is an extraordinarily competent, highly regarded young woman. It's not a case of one colleague standing up for another. I've been known to go for the jugular on occasions … but she's not one I can fault. If I was ever in an emergency, I'd want her looking after me—she enjoys that kind of reputation.'

Wells needed to know more about the Farah Jama debacle. He needed some clarity. The first thing he did was pay Detective Porter a visit. 'I don't understand,' he said to her. "Tell me how something like this can happen.' How could Jama be convicted when the evidence so obviously didn't stack up? Well, the jury found him guilty, was all Porter could say.

I tried to imagine her turbulent thoughts at this time. What more could she have done? She had asked the question about contamination. Granted, she had only asked about the possibility of contamination in the police lab. But she wasn't to know both women had passed through the same rape crisis unit, she wasn't alert to all the possible permutations that might give rise to contamination, she wasn't a scientist. She asked what was, from her limited perspective, the prudent question. She received a reply that so rang with certainty: 'I do not think contamination between the two cases could have occurred' … She had no reason to investigate further. Perhaps if the case manager at forensics, Deborah Scott, had been moved to sift through all the documentation relating to the two samples, the common link may have come to light. But what more could *she, Porter*, have done?

Now Wells' thoughts turned to Maria. The scandal would soon be all over the media. Yesterday she was a rape victim trying to get past a trauma. Tomorrow she would feel like a character in a tragic comedy—relieved, though more than a little humiliated. Wells felt he owed her a proper explanation. He wanted to look her in the eye and take responsibility for the catastrophic mistake. The Institute's lawyers told him to do no such thing. But the lawyers could go jump, he thought. Wells asked Maria to meet him at a cafe. It was urgent, he said.

Without Maria's input, what happened next is rather hard to decipher. Wells, who took a female colleague with him, remembers Maria being shocked by the news. I would regard this as an entirely reasonable reaction if I didn't know about her earlier, highly charged, meeting with Sonnet. Maria already knew the case was being re-opened amid serious doubts about Jama's conviction. However, Wells insists she gave no inkling of having been forewarned of any trouble.

I tried to slot this detail into my hazy profile of a woman I'll probably never meet. 'A very private person' was how someone described her. I have a vague sense of her as someone inclined to denial as a coping mechanism. She ignored my oblique letters, sent to her work address, which indicated that I would follow up with a phone call if I didn't receive a response. I would be following up just to make sure she received the letter—that's how I had put it, anyway. She then ignored my telephone messages. Yet she could have easily turned me away with a simple letter or an email: *'I don't wish to be interviewed. Please don't contact me again'*.

I knew enough to know she would be anxious about being inadvertently identified in my book. Her behaviour suggested someone so paralysed with anxiety she struggled to face up to reality. Had a similar response kicked in after her meeting with Sonnet? Had she wiped from her memory the very idea of Jama's innocence?

Wells and Maria talked over a range of issues in the café; Maria conceded that mistakes can happen. She was articulate and insightful, Wells said.

She was all those adjectives again—articulate, insightful, intelligent, dignified.

She expressed 'genuine grief' about Jama. The Institute's lawyers needn't have worried; she wouldn't be seeking compensation. As far as she was concerned, it was case closed forever.

On the Friday afternoon, Sonnet rang Patrick Tehan QC, Jama's new barrister, and asked him to amend his client's appeal to include two more grounds that would allow an acquittal, as opposed to merely a re-trial. He said the Crown was eager to bring the case on as soon as possible.

When this news reached Jama's solicitor, Kimani Boden, he was understandably surprised. Delighted, yes, but surprised. He then had what would surely rank as one of the most pleasing conversations of his career in breaking the news to his client.

'What were the reverberations like around here?' I asked Sonnet at our first meeting in his Lonsdale Street office. Hours had passed, during which I let my mobile ring out several times. Only later did I notice the day beginning to fade.

'Reverberations here?' He smirked, blushing slightly, and glanced at the OPP's media chief, who was sitting with us and seemed similarly entranced by Sonnet's narration.

'I'm looking at my guard dog here,' he said.

Well, it was tricky. His controversial appointment as Associate Crown Prosecutor was still a source of discontent in some quarters. Now here was the lowliest Associate 'Crownie', the one with a question mark over his credentials, saying senior people had gravely erred. Of course, Silbert supported him 'one hundred per cent' and Rapke trusted his judgment, too. He had plenty of backing from people who mattered, but others in the office did not support his conclusion. On that same Friday one Crown Prosecutor went so far as to call on him to relinquish his position. In front of everyone, the man called on Sonnet to stand down.

I sat up, startled.

'Look, there is a genuine principle at stake,' said Sonnet, in an effort to sound conciliatory. 'It risks undermining the whole system if people regularly seek to re-visit a jury verdict by asserting that a convicted man is innocent.'

'Were these other people involved in the original trial?' I asked.

'Ah ... I'd better not say. Let's just say there wasn't a universal opinion. Others held the view that Jama was plainly guilty.'

So some people, intelligent people, lawyers, still thought Jama 'plainly guilty'.

I had embarked on this journey with every faith in the system, believing the Farah Jama case no more than a regrettable instance of injustice, just one of those things that happen. Just one of those mistakes that get exposed eventually, to the mortification and profuse contrition of all the otherwise sensible and good-hearted people involved.

Sonnet's explanation that his outraged colleagues were defending the integrity of our legal system seemed plausible. What threw me was Sonnet's inclusion of the word 'plainly', and everything that implied: the unshakeable certainty, the emphatic absence of doubt even in the face of compelling evidence to the contrary.

It again made me question my long-held belief that the justice system was vacuum-sealed in reason.

※

'How soon can you convene a Court of Appeal?' Sonnet pressed the registrar on the Friday. His request was novel, but so were the circumstances. Farah Jama is an innocent man, Sonnet explained, they had to get an acquittal straight away. The registrar said he could list the case for Monday before Chief Justice Marilyn Warren, and Justices Robert Redlich and Bernard Bongiorno.

On Sunday 6 December 2009, Sonnet went in to the office and typed the Crown's submissions, largely replicating his memo to Silbert, in preparation for the appeal proceedings. Then he went home, bracing himself for the firestorm of the next day.

Chapter 22

On the way home from my visit to Loddon gaol in Castlemaine, the visit that took place in 2011 a few months after I met Jama, my partner, kindly acting as my driver for the day, stopped at a red light near Reservoir Station. Gazing out the window, I noticed a sign for Edwardes Street, home to the pool hall Edward's Place, the scene of *the night before*. The billiard hall, nestled in a suburban shopping strip, was a beacon for council workers and all manner of locals; a quirky place, somewhat uncertain of its identity. The front third hosted a licensed bar with tables facing the footpath, while the middle resembled an Italian-style cafe, replete with gelati bar. The billiard hall itself occupied the fairly large back section. I saw game machines, a couple of couches and a mirror ball hanging from the ceiling. I also saw a back door, which, we would soon learn, led to the car park. An attractive middle-aged woman was working near the gelati counter. My partner and I introduced ourselves. I explained I was writing a book that touched on an incident that took place here five years earlier, on 14 July 2006. Perhaps she was around at that time and could tell me what she remembered about that Friday night? She replied that yes, she was around back then, but that I had better speak to Sam, her husband. Sam, bald and muscular, was pulling beers with ruthless efficiency. I got the impression of someone tightly wound. The woman murmured something to him. He shot us a glance and kept working. There was a relaxed vibe in the late afternoon, the drinkers mainly blue-collar workers in overalls. Someone called Dianne dropped in, and then a Frankie. Sam gave each a cheerful welcome, along with their usual. We ordered some tea, waiting. I was beginning to feel uncomfortable, when Sam finally came to our table, shook hands and asked how he could help. So I began to explain. Farah Jama and wrongful rape conviction … At first Sam shook his head, then stopped, then said yes, maybe that rang a bell. Perhaps Sam remembered an incident that took place here on a Friday night involving a young woman and some Somali blokes? The police most likely turned up the next day or the next week to ask questions.

Again, Sam shook his head and then stopped. Yes, now he remembered. 'Oh, yeah, that girl who was raped!'

'Well no,' I said. 'No, she wasn't. She just made a complaint, that's all. It went nowhere. But I'm presuming the police came asking about the men?'

'They just wanted the footage,' he said. The surveillance footage from the car park, Sam explained. He shook his head, frowning.

'There are stories I could tell you about *that* car park.' The situation had improved since authorities tightened the liquor licensing laws, but back then things were hairy. 'I didn't tell them which car it was,' Sam said of his dealings with the police. 'I didn't tell them,' he repeated, emphasising each word as if his loyalty to patrons was in question. 'But when they told me it was a red car, I knew the one they meant.' He leaned in, as if about to confide. 'I knew *that* little red car.' The car's owner, he explained, was a bit of a regular. No, he didn't know the guy's name. Still sees him every now and then. Anyway … that's really all he could remember.

And that's really all there is to report about my meeting with Sam save to note that my observation about his being tightly wound proved accurate. At this point in the conversation something in Sam snapped. He looked from me to my partner, alarm and anger sparked in equal measure. Perhaps he ought to have a lawyer present, he said. Perhaps he shouldn't be talking to us at all.

'Who are you anyway,' he growled. 'Do you have a card or something?' Of course he didn't need a lawyer, I said, snickering light-heartedly in an attempt to reassure. And, of course, here … I rummaged about in my bag … well, I didn't have a card on me, but here was a national media pass. I pulled out a monstrously large laminated thing with a photograph, pointed to the big shiny stamp of accreditation, stuttered about how official this was, how no less than the Federal Government had authorised it. Sam scanned the frighteningly official-looking pass, his eyes darkening. Did he think I was a cop too? Or the Feds? Or ASIO? Abruptly, he stood up. 'I'm sorry,' I stammered. 'Did I say something to offend you?'

'You,' Sam barked, jabbing his finger in the air. 'You offended me by laughing in my face.'

He stormed back to the bar. For a moment my partner and I sat staring at one another, uncertain. I thanked Sam again for his time, he gave me a dismissive wave and we left Edward's Place, our knees wobbling.

At the time I judged this visit to the pool hall a success overall. At least now I was aware of the existence of video footage that showed Jama and others getting into a red car with a woman whose identity was still a mystery to me. (Only later did I learn that the footage came up blank.) Tracking down Taylah, the young woman from the pool hall, was always going to be difficult. Having encountered numerous roadblocks early on, I grew pessimistic of ever learning her name, let alone hearing her version of the events of Friday 14 July 2006. I wanted to dissect the episode for reasons that went beyond its status as the primal scene in an intricate narrative, beyond the obvious fact that had Jama never met Taylah none of this would have happened, and beyond my own belief that even as a discrete chapter in a much larger story the encounter between these young people seemed freighted with irony and misunderstanding and our collective pathologies about sex. The deeper significance of the pool hall incident lies in the silence that shrouded it throughout Jama's ordeal. No one could talk about the incident and yet everyone was thinking about it, and as is often the case in such circumstances, people leap to flawed and damaging conclusions.

The report of Frank Vincent QC's inquiry into the Jama case gave a cursory account of the pool hall incident. The account did not mention that other men, besides Jama, had been involved in the sexual encounter with Taylah. It simply related that the night before the Doncaster incident Jama declined the opportunity to engage in penile intercourse with an 'apparently enthusiastic' young woman.

When I first read the report I knew little else about the incident. I grappled with how a woman of such enthusiasm ends up in a rape crisis unit the very same night. Who had attested to her 'enthusiasm', I wondered. Perhaps Jama himself?

After a series of errant, throwaway remarks and subtle hints from numerous individuals, I finally confirmed that the sexual encounter in the back seat of the car had been a free-for-all. The information led me to hypothesise on some of the more obscure episodes of the Jama saga. For instance, I believed I had figured out why the police wanted forensic biologist Deborah Scott to perform a separate statistical calculation about the DNA evidence, using the Somali population. At trial, Scott said she carried out the analysis for the sake of 'rigour'.

But with Detective Karen Porter refusing to speak to me, I became convinced the police, being clearly aware of Taylah's allegations from the night before, asked for the Somali calculation on the off-chance someone might challenge the DNA match to Jama by raising the possibility that the sample could be attributed to one of his friends.

Above all, the salacious twist bolstered my theory about Jama's reluctance to tell his family, and possibly even his lawyers, the whole truth about the night before. After all, spilling the beans would also have meant outing his friends for taking part in unseemly antics.

In the process of fitting all the pieces together, I also learned a new word: bukkake, a term originating from porn culture. I was in the chambers of a criminal law barrister. We had been chatting about the 'lessons', from the legal profession's point of view, to emerge from the Jama case, when we veered off on a tangent. The barrister fished for a definition of the term online.

'Variety of fetish that involves repeated ejaculation on a female by many men,' he read from Urban Dictionary.

'And here it says, "Some authors have argued that *bukkake* involves the implied or overt humiliation of the person ejaculated upon".' He turned to face me, eyebrows raised studiously above his spectacles. 'So there's an element of contempt built into it.'

I later discovered that an earlier draft of the Vincent report contained a fuller account of the pool hall incident. That draft had been edited at the behest of counsellors from Centres Against Sexual Assault (CASA) to 'protect' Taylah. Though in reality she was already well protected. She may have withdrawn her police complaint, but the law still forbade me to identify her. By contrast, the young men who were in the car have no such privileges and the imbalance disturbed me.

If a rape complainant is entitled to anonymity in the wider domain, wouldn't basic fairness demand the same right be extended to the accused until a conviction is secured? Should I be allowed to expose these men for a teenage indiscretion they might well look back on with acute embarrassment, if not remorse? To which another voice responds, if these young men wish to keep their sex acts private they ought to beware of young women who appear up for everything and everyone. Real life seldom pans out like a porn flick.

In his 2010 *Age* interview, Jama gave a brief description of Taylah's conduct after the sexual encounter in the car. He did not mention, and the journalist did not know, about the involvement of the other men. Jama recalled in the interview that when it was over, Taylah had simply said good bye, 'like a normal person'. This made me scoff even before I knew the whole story of that night. What else could the young woman do but say good bye, like a 'normal person', affect an unruffled composure, a cool attitude? I had been there. Not fooling around in a car with three men, granted, but pretending to shrug off an encounter turned sour.

I could walk some way in Taylah's shoes. I understood her dissociative state during that short 'goodbye', when she emerged from the car splattered with semen, her initial lust presumably unsatisfied, if not deliberately mocked, her dignity shredded.

There are some secrets women still harbour, out of a twisted pride perhaps, or cowardice or self-hatred or guilt. They still prefer not to talk about the thin line between feeling desired and feeling degraded. About the sinking, scary moment when a sexual encounter slips from their control. If such encounters were a movie you would walk out or press the 'stop' button. But for all the Go-Girl! noise, for all the decades of feminist and sexual revolution, so many women remain mute.

A friend, a woman of volcanic intelligence, once confided about an episode involving an erstwhile male friend. The two of them had been smoking dope one night and she had had a bad reaction. She felt faint, began throwing up. The bloke, for whom she had neither felt nor feigned any attraction, chose that instant to make a pass.

'And I thought to myself, "You fucking bastard. Look at me, I've just thrown up",' she said.

'So what did you do?' I asked.

'I wouldn't let him touch me and just gave him a head job.'

Looking back, I now reckon the worst part of the story was my reaction. I nodded. We both nodded and sighed, as if my friend's response required no further explanation. This is what young women so often do. They are rarely sore losers. They play it cool when they feel they've been played, deliver blow jobs and say good bye, 'like a normal person'.

Only in this instance Taylah bucked expectation, calling in the umpire. Repulsed and outraged, she went to the police.

I asked the police if they might contact Taylah on my behalf, to let her know I was writing this book and wished to hear her perspective. My request was put to the lead detective on the investigation, and he responded with a firm 'no'.

He believed 'that any contact with the woman will most likely have detrimental effects on her wellbeing'. Nor was the detective willing to discuss the file with me.

'I am satisfied this was a false allegation of rape,' a lawyer who had read Taylah's file told me.

'Isn't "false allegation" a rather strong term?' I said. 'I mean, isn't that the kind of term you'd use for, say, someone maliciously lying, a fantasist, an allegation of rape where there was no sexual encounter whatsoever?'

'Okay, maybe "false" is a bit strong. But it's clear, reading between the lines, that the police believed she would not have been viewed as a witness of truth. Now that's just a legal term. It doesn't mean she's a liar, it just means you can't put her in front of a jury and say, "you can believe every word".'

The inconsistencies between her accounts were just too dramatic.

'She voluntarily had gone out [to the car], there was other evidence suggesting she had wanted to have sex with black men, she was intrigued, there were offers of money and all that …'

'Offers of money?' I gaped.

'Well, apparently there was a dare from a friend—something like, I'll give you fifty dollars or something if you fuck a black man.'

Taylah's second police statement, which I had the opportunity to read about a year after this discussion with the lawyer, referred only to a bet made between her friends about how long she'd last without sex. The lawyer's memory was probably hazy, but the conversation in his office alarmed me.

Who is this woman, I wondered? A distasteful image began taking shape: bogan-gone-wild, feral child, messy as hell.

'Look, he [Jama] didn't get charged,' the lawyer continued. 'That speaks volumes in a climate where if a victim makes a statement, most are charged now. I mean, we've completely changed … now if a victim makes a complaint of rape it's highly unusual for a prosecution not to be launched.'

We've completely changed. I kept brushing up against this theme, and on this much at least everyone agrees. We've changed utterly from the days when rape victims tended not to be believed, when they could be cross-examined about their intimate lives, when they had to endure a 'medical' at Russell Street police station against the background noise of drunks and louts being locked up for the night.

The debating point is whether we've changed too much, gone too far 'the other way'. For a while I allowed myself to get sucked into this vortex.

The team for the affirmative, comprising many defence barristers and other lawyers, argue the pendulum has swung too far in the other direction so that the system is now skewed in favour of alleged victims. One pointed refrain of the 'yes' team is that these days almost every woman who alleges rape gets her day in court. The prosecutors will take on almost every rape case even when they know the chances of securing a conviction are slim.

We let juries do the hard work, claims the affirmative team—we leave it to them to sort out who's lying and who's telling the truth. Even though more often than not the jury throws the case out, the whole *raison d'etre* of the sexual offences unit in the OPP is to enable victims to take a stand. Accuse prosecutors of a 'jihad mentality' and they would probably take it as a compliment. And to be fair, the legislation from Spring Street, laden with motherhood statements and guiding principles—*'courts … should have regard to the fact that there is a high incidence of sexual violence within society'*, and the like—envisages no less.

Not to mention the media circus around rape cases, especially when the accused is a public figure. Only the most crazy-brave Director of Public Prosecutions could resist the pressure in such circumstances and decide not to proceed with the case. Think it strange the Jama case received so little scrutiny from prosecutors? Well, the affirmatives say, the same goes for sexual offences generally. To which the team for the negative, comprising many feminists, the former Attorney-General, the former Director of Public Prosecutions and others besides, say that's simply not true—the weak cases go nowhere or, depending on the perspective, still too many worthy cases culminate in a not guilty verdict and still too many other worthy cases don't even make it to the courtroom. And even if it is kind of true that almost every woman gets her day in court, as some in the team for the negative concede, the dinosaurs had better get with the times.

And then in September 2011, I saw an article in *The Age* reporting that a senior Victorian judge suggested that some accused sex offenders should be dealt with outside the traditional courts in a system similar to South Africa's truth and reconciliation commissions. In this scheme they would be forced to meet with the victim and hear her pain.

There was a time when I might have bristled at the idea as soft on sex offenders. Now I reckon it's the only hope of negotiating this treacherous chasm between the sexes, the irreconcilable he said, she said.

Let's sit around a table, look one another in the eye and start speaking the truth.

※

One afternoon of the same year, 2011, I found myself in the office of another lawyer with knowledge of Taylah's complaint. I was still angling for any scraps of information, but the man would have none of it.

'Now, I'm not talking about *that*,' he slapped me down. He was not interested in talking about all that 'silly stuff' regarding Jama's encounter with the woman the night before.

'That silly stuff?' I asked, incredulous.

'Silly stuff,' he repeated. The pool hall incident of the night before was largely irrelevant and I would be best advised to leave it alone, he said.

I prodded the lawyer to help me make sense of it all—a woman 'apparently enthusiastic' about sex, to use Vincent's words, ends up at a rape crisis unit. How? Why?

'She ends up at a rape crisis unit that night,' the lawyer eventually snapped, 'because she doesn't get what she wanted.'

I froze. Had I heard him correctly? A woman ends up at a rape crisis centre, not because of what was done to her, but because of what *wasn't* done. So badly had she wanted sex with these men and so profound her disappointment when they failed to deliver that she sought revenge through the law.

Was I being unfair, was my interpretation too literal? Was this man guilty of nothing more than a poor choice of words?

Perhaps. But to spin the story like that he'd have to be utterly ignorant of how a woman alone in a car with three aroused strangers might feel. This, despite all the gender education and feminist law reform and specialist sex offences units. In any event, I guess he was saying that I shouldn't be second-guessing the police for not laying charges over Taylah's allegations, that I shouldn't 'speculate.' Of course, I'd been speculating furiously about Jama's conduct and drawing adverse conclusions. Even after everything, I was on some level, shockingly, still ready to believe the worst of him. Yet surely this is precisely the point. Three men get sexual with one alcohol-affected woman in a car in a secluded street—the bare scenario evokes menace. At the least the scenario suggests a casual opportunism on the part of the men, an expectation that the woman will bend to the balance of power in the car. With nothing more to go on, surely most people would make adverse assumptions about the men. In all likelihood both the Defence and Prosecution, the barristers and the solicitors on both sides of the Jama trial, also knew this much, and only this much, about the night before. Surely it is reasonable to ask whether that knowledge tainted their perception of the accused.

When I learned of Taylah's 'Fuck me, fuck me!' outburst, the revelation finally laid to rest the question of why the police decided not to lay charges against the three men. Taylah in the witness box would be, to quote what Jama's counsel had said about the alibi witnesses, 'easy sport' for any defence barrister.

Then I saw it. Taylah's name. Buried in a legal document. I quickly found a Facebook profile that matched. And a MySpace profile and Twitter and you name it; there she was on just about every social networking site. Pictures of wild parties, captioned 'Hey, look at me blind! *As usual!*' Lists of her favourite blockbusters. Stream-of-consciousness diary entries, veering, without warning, between the sentimental, the patriotic, the vulgar, the reflective, the sad. Declarations of love one year, followed the next by a breezy 'Single again!' An entire life online.

And when this woman went for a ride with three strange men from the Edward's Place pool hall in 2006, she was already the mother of a toddler. This fact jolted me, probably because of the contrasts it threw up. Jama, and most likely the others too, still living at home with their mothers, tip-toeing around the taboos and secrets. And this child, already a mother herself.

At a beery pool hall their disparate lives collided.

A rape crisis counsellor from CASA thought I ought to be aware of a thing or two before I tried to contact Taylah. The utmost sensitivity was called for in these circumstances, she stressed during one of many phone conversations. She had also declined to make an approach to Taylah on my behalf.

While sympathetic to my professed desire to give the young woman a 'voice' in the story, for reasons of confidentiality she couldn't really help.

Still, if the Facebook profile indeed belonged to the woman I was looking for—a fact she could neither confirm nor deny—then she had some general advice to offer. She said it was general advice, although I knew she had been looking at Taylah's file only the day before. It was a rather oblique conversation; pregnant, or so I thought, with clues.

'You see, Julie, what you ought to know about the women we tend to see here … you see the kind of women who tend to be targeted … usually have a history of sexual abuse. You know some of them may have been abused since they were five, that kind of thing. And they've often got mental health problems, substance-abuse problems.'

And this woman, the counsellor said, might be totally ignorant of the Farah Jama scandal or the Vincent report or indeed new titles in bookstores. She might well be 'the sort of person' who was unlikely to know anything at all about what she had started on July 14.

I sent a curt but polite Facebook message, saying I was a journalist writing a book and wished to speak with her about it. Within five minutes came a slightly husky voice message on my mobile. She wanted to know what my 'random' message was about. I rang back and explained I was writing about the case of a Somali man called Farah Jama, though I wasn't sure if the name meant anything to her. A few years ago, I said, this man was wrongly convicted of a serious offence on DNA evidence. And the reason why the police had his DNA in the first place was because of an incident involving her.

'I think I know the incident you mean,' said the husky voice.

An intelligent and polite voice; the voice of a 'normal person'.

She said the incident took place many years ago. 'But I dropped it, it didn't go any further'.

I said that actually the matter did go further. She said she didn't know that. She agreed it was best we meet up so I could take her through the developments, which I had intimated were 'bizarre'. We made a date for me to drive to country Victoria to see her. The call over, I snorted at those precious counsellors with their 'victims this' and 'victims that', all this 'detrimental to her well-being' bullshit. Why do the do-gooders insist on infantilising those whose rights they champion?

Five minutes later Taylah sent a text message. Could we please put off our meeting until she'd spoken to her counsellor and was sure she was 'strong enough mentally'? She hoped I understood her feelings. I left it a month and rang her again. 'Sorry, who are you?' she asked. Oh yeah, she remembered now. Well, she had to consult her counsellor some more.

A few days later she rang me to say I could drive down to see her on 14 November. It wasn't ideal, but I wasn't about to negotiate. When the fourteenth arrived she cancelled just as my keys were turning in the ignition. Her 'support person' was sick, she said in a text message. We had to make another time.

So we settled on another date. As the date approached with no word from her, I started to think that maybe this time she'd follow through. Still, all the talk of 'support' people and counsellors had me worried. Was she likely to fold at the first prickly question, shatter like delicate porcelain? How to explain my growing nervousness? It eventually dawned on me that I was starstruck. She was, after all, a major protagonist in this story and at last I would be setting eyes on her.

The girl with semen in her hair.

Chapter 23

My doubts about Taylah persisted even as I drove to our rendezvous, barely registering the changing scenery as the city receded. Arriving a few minutes late at a shopping complex that looked as if it had been dumped from the sky on the side of a flat and empty landscape dissected by roads, I searched for the designated café, which the locals told me was 'round the back, next to the car park'. Scanning the cluster of outside diners, I stopped at two women, one younger, one older, chatting over empty plates. As I approached, the younger woman came into focus. I saw a face with enough resemblance to the Facebook photographs I had pored over. Our eyes locked and she nodded. She gave a hesitant smile.

She was slender, with auburn hair resting on her shoulders in two thick plaits. She wore a black and white paisley skirt, thongs and a black, scooped-neck sleeveless top with holes that made a lacy pattern just above the bust-line. Her crooked teeth suggested there had been no spare change in her childhood for orthodontic bills. In fact, I would soon learn she had been brought up by a single mother, and knew nothing at all about her father.

'He could have been one of about seven blokes,' she'd shrugged. 'I mean, just pick a name out of a hat.'

Teeth aside, I saw a china doll face, with creamy, flawless skin. The pretty face of a person I immediately sensed as courteous and obliging.

Her 'support person' was a short-haired, round-bodied, middle-aged woman. Precisely how old, I couldn't tell, but she was quite possibly younger than she looked. Having just 'knocked off' she was dressed in her work uniform: a navy blue polo-necked T-shirt with a petrol station logo. A small pair of purple earrings with silver trimming was her only adornment. She sucked hard on her cigarette.

'I'm Leanne,' she said, shooting an edgy sideways glance.

I sat down and again thanked Taylah for meeting me. I asked if it was still the case that she didn't know what happened, didn't know why I was here. She confirmed she knew nothing aside from the vague account I had given her.

'Well, I'm sorry, there's no gentle way into this,' I began.

So I took her back to the early hours of 15 July 2006, when she complained to the police and underwent a rape exam. Taylah nodded. And she probably recalled the doctor snipping a bit of her hair that was stuck together with semen? Taylah nodded.

And for a while, as I leapt through the narrative—from contamination of Maria's sample to Jama's conviction, to his release, to his compensation package, to his professed wish to make a book and film of his experiences—Taylah kept nodding. Then at a certain point she stopped nodding and just listened. Leanne—apparently an old family friend who had known Taylah since she was a little girl—made the odd comment here and there, but otherwise blew smoke into the air and tilted her head away, her expression non-committal.

The narrative came to an end. Leanne scrunched her mouth, raised her eyebrows and drew a deep breath. She said nothing. Taylah looked at me blankly.

After a few moments I asked for her reaction. She answered in a stiff, formal voice.

'Well, I mean, it wasn't very fair. It wasn't very fair to him. Because he didn't do it.'

'But what about ya feelings?' Leanne piped up, emphatic. 'Don't just say what ya think you should say. Tell us how ya really feel.'

Taylah wriggled on her chair. 'C'mon tell us,' Leanne urged. 'Okay,' Taylah relented. 'When you first said he went to gaol, I thought, "Woohoo!"' Her voice bounced with glee. 'And then I thought, "Well, *he's* copped it, but why should the others get off scot-free? Every dog has its day".'

Taylah recounted the events as best she could. Where her recollection was patchy her police reports helped fill in some of the gaps even after I discounted the contentious parts of her initial statement.

That weekend, she had left her son in the care of her mother. She went to stay with her old school-friend, Ella, in Reservoir. On Friday night, about four or five friends—

young men and women—knocked back some Jim Beams. She was pretty drunk, but not high. Like Ella, she's totally against drugs. She's seen up close the devastation they can cause.

She thought it rather ironic that she was actually dressed modestly that night—black pants, black top with three-quarter-length sleeves. In those days she tended to run round in skimpy dresses, only she had just returned from a stint in Queensland and felt the cold for a change. Kicked out of home at sixteen, she'd moved from town to town, from state to state, from refuge to refuge, messing up and starting afresh.

She was bubbly and talkative that Friday, '… but that's my mood every day'. At the billiard hall, she played a few games of pool and got talking to 'a black guy'. He had short, scruffy-looking hair and gave his name as 'Abs'. He told her he was African-American. He suggested they go somewhere else, 'for more drinks or something'. Ella tried to stop her, but she liked the idea of a 'cruise around' with this man.

'Were you prepared to have sex with him?' I asked.

'Yeah,' she said, off-hand. 'From memory, I thought he was a pretty nice guy … pretty good looking. I agreed to go with *him*. I didn't realise there were others until we got in the car.'

In her first police statement, Taylah said she and Abs had walked to a red car out the back of the pool hall when another man, dressed in white and cream, arrived on the scene and began chatting to her. The man explained he was the driver, and took his seat behind the wheel, as she and Abs climbed into the back together. A moment before they drove off, a third man in a red shirt jumped into the front passenger seat.

I tried to challenge her assertion of a quasi-ambush, suggesting a casual onlooker might have seen her climbing into the vehicle without a moment's hesitation. In all likelihood, she was revising history. Then again, my own 'decisions' at nineteen would fast dissolve under cross-examination. It is the age of vaguely feeling the danger and doing it anyway.

In the intervening years, Taylah had convinced herself there had been four guys in the car, not three. She was wrong, her memory blurred the details. But she had felt hemmed in, trapped; that was the point. The unpleasant flashbacks had a man on either side of her, a man at the wheel. Nowadays she couldn't remember what any of the guys looked like.

I showed her a picture of Jama.

'That's the guy whose semen was in your hair,' I said.

'Look, there could have been semen from four guys in my hair,' she shook her head. 'I was covered in semen from hair to waist. There was a lot of it. The cops said there was heaps on my top. A few months later, they sent a package with my clothes to my grandma's house and I thought, "*Ooh*, why would I want that?"'

'That stuff belongs in ponds!' Leanne quipped.

Through all this, Leanne had been coming out with gags and anecdotes. About numerous colourful characters around town. About her husband, who she insisted was a 'virgin'. 'Now, you'd know this,' she said to me at one stage. How could she find out whether someone had been released from prison?

I tried to filter out Leanne's light relief, but the mood was turning ribald. Even I hazarded a joke about Taylah's clothes hardly being something you might want to flog on eBay. This wasn't Monica Lewinsky's dress, after all. Taylah giggled. As she lit a cigarette, I noticed traces of purple varnish on her fingernails.

The two other guys were introduced as Abs' cousins, 'Casey' and 'CJ'. At times the guys talked among themselves 'in their own language'. They drove to a quiet street and parked the car at the tennis courts, driving right up to the fence. A street lamp cast only a dim light, the fence resembled a cage.

'And that's when the event happened,' Taylah winced.

She made the first move. This she admitted to the police straight up. Started kissing Abs, fooled around with him. She had Abs's penis in her mouth when the man in the red shirt joined them in the back, shifting her to the middle. She closed her eyes. Someone pulled her pants down to her ankles. When Abs was finished he moved to the front, and the driver took his place in the back.

She remembered hands at the back of her head, moving it up and down rhythmically. Men kneeling on the seat. Her giving oral sex to the driver, then to the man in the red shirt, then to the driver again, as Abs leaned over from the front seat, his fingers inside her. She felt a cool, gel-like substance sprayed between her legs. Swallowing and dry-retching, again and again and again. She moved. Some cum shot into her hair.

'I was just numb, just thinking, "Get me out of here!"'

'Yet, you yelled out, "Fuck me, fuck me!",' I challenged her.

'Yeah,' Taylah replied, nonchalant. 'I know I'm weird like that. But for me, oral has always been a lot more personal.'

So she was ready to have vaginal sex with all three guys?

She gave a heavy, defeatist sigh. 'Well … I'm just saying, I would have rather done *that* than oral.'

So these teenage boys had the police come knocking because they failed at psychoanalysis. Because they failed to decipher her yelling, 'Fuck me, fuck me!', actually meant 'Get me the fuck out of here', because they failed to see through her show of enthusiasm.

When the encounter finished, Taylah asked the men to let her out down the street from the pool hall. Before she got out of the car, Abs asked if she was okay. 'Yeah I'll be alright,' she replied and walked back to Ella's place, where she fell apart.

'You gave the police a version of events that left out important details,' I said. Hadn't she deliberately distorted the truth to make the men appear culpable?

'Yeah,' she said, with a slight toss of the head. Though she had also genuinely forgotten certain details on the first telling, her memory was selective, alcohol skewed things.

The medical exam was 'pretty scary, pretty daunting'. When Cunningham snipped her locks she had a girly 'Oh no! Not my hair!' moment. Otherwise, 'like every other victim, I just wanted to get into the shower'.

The following week she went to police headquarters on St Kilda Road to give another statement to officers from the Sexual Crimes Squad. She distinctly remembered a male officer infuriating her.

'I just didn't like the way he was talking to me. He asked me things like, "Why didn't you scream?" and I said, "Well, have you ever been so scared that you can't scream?" I think someone in that kind of position should show more *empathy*, they should be more *compassionate*.'

Her china doll eyes widened with each emphasis, her tone haughty.

The officer pissed her off so badly she demanded to talk to another police officer, who she knew also worked at 'St Kilda'. This other police officer had helped her with a previous sexual abuse complaint against the son of a family friend, an ordeal that had gone on for years. I thought of Ella's casual mention of having been raped on the way to school. The police refused Taylah's request for the other officer to handle matters, and the officer she had found objectionable kept pursuing the case once she returned home to the country. She began to feel hassled. He demanded answers, wanted the file wrapped up. Taylah now insisted he fit in with her schedule. After ten days, she withdrew her complaint, realising that if the matter had progressed to court she would end up looking worse than the three men. The 'Fuck me, fuck me!' outburst would inevitably unravel her case.

'I woulda just screamed,' said Leanne.

'I thought, if I scream something worse can happen … Especially with them being of a different nationality as well. You don't know what their moral ideas are, how they treat their women.

'I end up dead in the gutter and I'm a mother, and my son would have to deal with that. I mean I *actually* thought about my son'—a fact she considered especially poignant because back then she rarely acknowledged her maternal responsibilities—'… and well, there's a lot of racism here, it's very racist, and he might take it out on innocent people.'

How many roles was she playing now? The rape victim rendered passive by fear, the cultural theorist on ethnicity and gender politics, the humanitarian concerned her ending up 'dead in the gutter' might provoke her son to racist retribution? I worried she was feeding me the lines she thought I wanted to hear.

The police had concluded Taylah would not have made 'a witness of truth'. 'Suggestible', was how I'd eventually describe her. Attuned, to an almost unnerving degree, to the wishes of others. To be fair, though, I had been asking her some leading questions.

'I suppose,' I said, of her complicated psychological state in the car that night, 'you say to yourself, "Well, now that I've started this, I have to finish it".'

'That's right,' she said.

Fragments from nasty episodes of my youth surfaced like scum. I thought again about my friend and her blow-job administered in anger.

Taylah said she had only recently 'dealt with' the incident through her friendship with an African guy at her college. (She fell pregnant in Year 11, left school and had only recently returned to study, pursuing a qualification in Community Services.) She had explained with a nervous chuckle during our first phone-call that this man 'brought up my issues with dark men'. At the time I was struck by how her words echoed Maria's reference to taxi drivers of the 'dark' persuasion.

The African man at the college opened her mind to the horrors of war and the hardships faced by refugees, and also to cultural differences, 'their strict rules about women, having three wives, things like that…'

'Why can't I 'ave three husbands?' Leanne whined. 'I want three husbands!'

We chuckled. Leanne went on, 'That's one thing I think they ought to teach them at these internment camps—about cultural differences, about how, "You do things this way, but this is how we do it".'

Taylah had also covered 'cultural diversity' in her course work and these days had a much greater appreciation of such matters. At first she was reluctant to accept a ride from her African friend. She would insist on sitting next to the door to allow for a speedy escape. Being in a car with black guys was a 'trigger', she said, explaining that her counsellor had trained her to deal with incidents that reminded her of trauma. But then she overcame her irrationality, worked out how to judge everyone as an individual.

'And I'm proud of you for that,' said Leanne, warmly, 'because it's got nothin' to do with skin colour. White boys do stuff like that, too.'

'Lots of racism here,' said Taylah again, doleful, as her eyes swept the pavement, and the car park, emptier now than when I arrived.

The two women lit up and leant back in their chairs, relaxed; Leanne the raconteur, Taylah her adoring audience. Leanne persisted with the gags, Taylah shook with laughter till her eyes watered. For all the effort it had taken me to drag them here, they seemed in no hurry to leave.

But exhaustion, and a weird sense of disorientation, had overtaken me. The long drive home was still ahead. I insisted on paying for their lunch, even though they'd eaten before I came. I forced Taylah's limp hand into mine and shook it. She recoiled slightly and dropped her eyes to the table.

Chapter 24

On Monday 7 December 2009, the Farah Jama case was listed in the Court of Appeal. At 9.30 am, Sonnet rose to his feet before the three justices to tell them of the likely contamination of a DNA sample that resulted in a 'substantial miscarriage of justice'.

His 'opponent', Jama's counsel, was Patrick Tehan QC, most striking for his imperial-style curled moustache. As appeal hearings typically hinge on doctrinal questions of law it is commonplace for solicitors to call in the heavy guns on their client's behalf and brief a silk, a senior barrister whose hefty daily fee is but one mark of their skill. The fund-raising efforts of the Somali community presumably enabled the same calculation to be made in the Jama case, although by this Monday it was clear the appellant would leave the courtroom with an order, among others, that he be indemnified for legal expenses. Indeed, this appeal would rank as the easiest of Tehan's decades-long career. Seated at the bar table, he could do little else but listen intently to his opponent's address.

In the end, Sonnet caved in to colleagues and stopped short of declaring Jama 'innocent' before the court and all the world. A storm was unleashed all the same. After the three justices declared they were 'satisfied' from the Crown's submissions that it was 'appropriate to order' the original conviction be set aside and a verdict of acquittal entered, Jama and his solicitor, Kimani Boden, gave their triumphant media door-stop outside the court. They posed for the cameras with their arms draped round one another's shoulders, Jama looking dazed and characteristically defiant, Boden beaming on what he described as a 'momentous' day.

Jama briefly addressed reporters. He said he felt 'angry and depressed'. What happened to him was 'very, very bad'.

By virtue of necessity, Sonnet managed to dodge the scrum. The appeal over, he had to stay in the courtroom for a different case that took nearly three hours. The reporters hung around for a while, waiting for him to materialise, and then got sick of it. When he emerged at lunchtime, he was greeted by a solitary photographer.

Back at his chambers, staff at the OPP were in a frenzy. The media officer was beside herself, a mountain of phone messages awaited. The judges' associates from the Court of Appeal rang to say their switchboards were in meltdown. The press demanded interviews! Answers! Documents! Sonnet released a truncated version of the Crown's submissions. He had been told to be careful. There would be a claim for compensation down the track, it was all a little sensitive.

In another office in the same building, the state's chief prosecutor, Director of Public Prosecutions Jeremy Rapke QC, was working furiously at damage control. The legal experts and civil libertarians were already taking to the airwaves, criticising prosecutors for failing to warn jurors bedazzled by 'the CSI-effect'—the portrayal of forensic science in pop culture, including the eponymous TV franchise—of the limitations of DNA evidence.

'They see television shows,' one lawyer said on TV, 'and the television shows fix everything in an hour, and they say that DNA's the be-all and end-all of the case.'

Rapke decreed that in future cases based solely on DNA evidence would need his authorisation to proceed.

At Spring Street, the Attorney-General Rob Hulls received a briefing on the miscarriage of justice that would lead the day's news. He had barely processed the scale of the debacle before he decided to announce an official inquiry. He had in mind for the job, retired Supreme Court judge Frank Vincent QC, a veteran of about two hundred murder trials and a 'hard evidence' man not known for sparing feelings. The scandal made it onto the agenda of the morning's cabinet meeting. The ministers agreed that Vincent was their man.

The Institute of Forensic Medicine was forced to take the heat. Professor Cordner fronted a press conference alone to issue a *mea culpa*. He announced a review of the Institute's protocols. Of all the agency chiefs and individuals who contributed to the injustice, he was the only one who publicly apologised to Jama.

At Macleod and at the Victoria Police headquarters, a gloom descended. The timing of the revelations was abysmal. Monday was just the start of what would turn into a tough week for Police Chief Commissioner Simon Overland. Deputy Police Commissioner Sir Ken Jones, once a rival of Overland for the top job, noted, rather unhelpfully after the fact, that in his native UK, police desisted from proceeding with cases based solely on DNA evidence.

For Overland, the Jama case was the latest in a series of headaches. The media seized on the scandal as 'the third case of DNA contamination in six years'. The Jaidyn Leskie bungle, the embarrassing withdrawal a year earlier of murder charges against Russell John Gesah over the Tapp killings, and now this. Triggered by the Gesah debacle, a police review of six thousand DNA cases turned up one possible instance of contamination between DNA evidence in a car theft and a cannabis case. Fortunately, no wrongful charges had been laid in that mix-up.

There were other problems too. The police laboratory had recently acquired some powerful new technology that could extract DNA from ever smaller samples. However, it also became apparent that a new, more conservative statistical model was needed to accurately interpret the results. The state's defence lawyers began pushing back, and rightly so. Overland recruited three international experts to help fix the problem, and once again hundreds of DNA samples in pending cases needed to be re-tested.

In the hiatus, prosecutions stalled. An armed robbery case was derailed. On the Wednesday following Jama's vindication, Overland announced to the media that in order to allow the experts to devise a new statistical model, all police scientists were banned for a month from giving DNA evidence in court. Now high-profile cases involving bikies gangs and gangland figures were also on ice. The tabloids foamed at the mouth.

If all this wasn't bad enough, the very next day the Victorian Ombudsman lashed the police laboratory's Drug and Alcohol Unit, for, among other things, keeping sensitive exhibits in open boxes and without tamper-proof seals.

None of this was strictly relevant to the Jama scandal, of course, given it was not after all an instance of contamination in the police lab. Its proximity to the week's other stories of the constabulary's woes simply enabled the media to paint with a somewhat broad brush.

Still, legal commentators and academics began slotting the case into a broader narrative about 'cultural problems' within the force. These voices would be stronger after the Vincent inquiry revealed the police lab had been asked about the possibility of contamination in Jama's case, only to dismiss with absolute certainty the suggestion of an error on their part. Police forensics received yet another rap on the knuckles from the former judge for failing to come clean about the fact, however inconsequential, that Deborah Scott had acted as case manager for the samples of both Taylah and Maria.

And the timing was charged for Melbourne's Somalis.

They were already smarting over the arrests four months earlier of three Somalis accused of plotting to attack a Sydney army base. (One of the three would be later found guilty of the offence.) They insisted the manner of the arrests—the storming of nineteen family homes, the media circus—was intended to humiliate and stigmatise the community. Federal Police attended a community forum in Coburg in a bid to mend relations. Only a few invitations had been sent out, but a hundred or so Somalis turned up to vent their outrage. They accused police of hyping the arrests to deflect criticism of their handling of a spate of attacks on Indian students.

Osman had told the media the terror suspects were innocent. He branded the police themselves 'terrorists' for not liaising with the community first, for waking families in the middle of the night at gunpoint. He posed unsmiling at his restaurant. The *Herald Sun* referred to him as someone who was 'until now a voice of moderation between Somalis and the wider community'.

Now there was another lightning rod, the Jama scandal, the news of an astonishing injustice inflicted on one of their young. Sheik Isse from Werribee mosque sought to reassure his flock. He told them that while justice was delayed, it had nevertheless come. The system worked—Somalis had to trust in the rule of law. But many weren't convinced. What was the Jama case if not proof, if not confirmation, of the police conspiracy against them? Sheik Isse watched, with sadness and concern, as his community 'psychologically withdrew'.

I had asked the Jamas' friend, Omar Farah, if the belief the police had deliberately fitted up the youth was widespread.

'Absolutely!' he replied.

His own wife routinely warned their son, 'Be careful when you are out and around. Remember that no matter what you do, you are black'.

⋈

The week was a triumphant one for Kimani Boden. He soaked up the adulation, he was everywhere the talking head. 'My trust has been shaken,' he said on the ABC's *7.30 Report*. It was difficult to imagine an error of this magnitude could occur in such a 'sophisticated society' as ours. Jama was a 'great guy'; what happened to him was a tragedy.

Boden's glory mutated as it spread, until even the likes of former High Court judge, Michael Kirby, credited him with having 'carefully traced' the incriminating sample to find the missing link that exonerated Jama. This was, of course, entirely inaccurate—the source of the sample's contamination had been a complete mystery to the Defence team right until Sonnet, on the eve of the appeal, had revealed all.

And the story itself spread and mutated, until Jama became Sudanese, until Maria's age at the time of the incident was forty in one report and fifty-something elsewhere, until the contamination was described as having occurred when Jama 'gave blood' in the same room a week before Maria's examination. The story blew over in two or so days, a mini-cyclone of outrage, leaving mild public chaos in its wake.

⋈

Frank Vincent QC, is the son of a wharfie. He carries with him the old man's baling hook, a totem that speaks of his journey from the gritty Port Melbourne of his childhood to his Judges' Chambers in the Supreme Court. Vincent Senior was an ardent trade unionist and a gifted orator; his wife was a factory worker, a florist and a one-time vaudeville dancer who taught her son tap. So in Vincent, as in Judge Lacava, we have a Catholic, working-class kid made good. The criminal law is full of them.

He has the face of an Aussie larrikin. Sunken cheeks, thin lips and dark, probing eyes that warn of a forensic mind and fiery temperament. He has a way of speaking out of the corner of his mouth with a sharp intake of breath, as if he's making a wry or ironic comment, which he often is.

His caustic and literary voice is heard in the report, released four months after the miscarriage of justice appeared on the front pages, and titled, 'The inquiry into the circumstances that led to the wrongful conviction of Mr Farah Abdulkadir Jama'. He compares the DNA evidence in the case to the broken statue of Ozymandias, found isolated in a vast desert, recounted in the poem by Shelley. The 'colossal wreck' depicted by the 19th century English poet has inscribed on its pedestal the words, 'My name is Ozymandias, king of kings: Look on my works, ye Mighty, and despair!' And just like this inscription, Vincent continues, everything around the DNA evidence 'belied the truth of its assertion':

> The statue, of course, would be seen by any reasonably perceptive observer, and viewed in its surroundings, as a shattered monument to an arrogance that now mocked itself.

By contrast, the DNA evidence appears to have been viewed as possessing an almost mystical infallibility that enabled its surroundings to be disregarded. The outcome was, in the circumstances, patently absurd.

The literary inevitably gives way to the earthy as Vincent summarises the Institute of Forensic Medicine's thinking on precisely how the crusting flakes of semen in Taylah's hair came to contaminate Maria's samples. Was it the scissors? Cunningham, the forensic medical officer, had snipped the end of the tubular sheath that contained Maria's swab with the same pair of scissors she used the day before to cut Taylah's hair. Probably not, the report concluded, otherwise how to explain the sperm on the slide, which was dabbed with Maria's swab *before* the tubular sheath was cut? Might the contamination have occurred in the common areas, occupied by Taylah one day and Maria the next; the couch and chair in the counselling room, the bathroom, the examination room? No, that's too vague an explanation.

According to the Vincent report, this is the most likely scenario:

In the early hours of Saturday, Cunningham examines Taylah. She takes swabs from the young woman, creates slides from those swabs. She cuts a portion of Taylah's hair and bags it for the police lab. A pre-stocked trolley has everything she needs within a hand's reach: scissors, a row of fresh slides, all of them uncovered. All the while the dried semen in Taylah's hair is shedding fragments on the scissors, the bed, the trolley. One of those fragments lands on the exposed surface of a slide, a slide that's next in line for use.

Mid-morning on Sunday, Cunningham attends the examination room once more, this time for Maria. The room hasn't been touched since she was last here. No one had come to clean or decontaminate the space, an omission of which the doctor is unaware.

She takes a swab of Maria's cervix. When the procedure is done, Cunningham places the elongated cotton bud back in its tubular sheath. From the uncovered, pre-stocked trolley she picks up a new slide, the same slide that from the previous night bears a speck of semen. She dabs the middle of the slide with Maria's cervical swab, transferring the semen from one to the other. Or perhaps it's actually the swab that has managed to collect a speck of semen from the surroundings and the semen is then smeared onto the slide.

Whatever the case, both the slide and the swab are now contaminated.

The former, viewed under the microscope in the police lab, reveals a sperm with a tail, the latter, once tested, is found to contain the DNA of Farah Jama.

It is a dark comedy of errors. A fragment of 'male seed', invisible to the naked eye, flutters onto a surface and, before long, multiple lives are thrust into chaos.

I visited the former judge at his office in the Victoria University Law School, in the heart of the legal district. He gave me a curt greeting, eyes magnified from behind his spectacles. He eschewed small talk. I opened with a question about whether the Jama case was the worst miscarriage of justice he'd seen, and soon the glasses came off and the story-telling began, along with the biting, occasionally combative, remarks and the wisecracks delivered from the side of the mouth.

You never tempt fate by bringing superlatives to travesty, Vincent said, but what struck him was the abject failure at every stage of the criminal justice system. We elaborated on themes from the report. The 'staggering' lack of curiosity from both the Defence and Prosecution about the contents of Jama's first police file—had anyone bothered to look at it, the connection between Taylah and Maria would likely have become apparent. How the Prosecution probably deserved the most criticism for its decision to proceed in the first place; how Judge Lacava's lack of experience in the area of DNA evidence meant the hard questions weren't tackled.

He talked about the alibi witnesses. About the self-defeating conduct of people so desperate to persuade that they exaggerate, becoming overly elaborate.

'I used to get this years ago with injured workers,' he said. 'They can, on a good day, get around, but they would go over the top and exaggerate their symptoms just to let you know how crook they were. But you don't just dismiss them because of that.

'Even telling lies; it's something you've got to assess very carefully. When I was on the Parole Board, one of the comments I used to make to prisoners in the gaol who were trying to convince me of their rehabilitation was, "I'm sorry, son, you're a long way off the pace: you haven't even identified the lies you ought to tell me!" Sometimes you need a lot of experience in determining what a lie actually says about a person.'

I, too, had known many a melodramatic compo claimant—factory workers who insisted on wearing a neck brace until the trial was done—and yet I rarely doubted their suffering was genuine. Granted, the issues in a regular workers' compensation trial, in which the fact of an injury, as opposed to its severity, was usually uncontested, bear little resemblance to the intellectual leap demanded of the jury by Jama's Defence team. The jurors, after all, were being asked to reject the implication of guilt in the DNA evidence, and put in its place a story that appeared, in the Prosecutor's words, 'cobbled together' and 'synthetic'.

All the same, it struck me as disheartening that I would likewise have drawn the most damaging conclusions from the theatrics of the alibi witnesses. My observations of human nature would have counted for nought.

The observation of Vincent's that most resonated was the trial lawyers' baffling lack of curiosity about the pool hall incident. The incident was the elephant in the courtroom, the answer to the 'inevitable' question. Yet, again and again, I read the transcript of the sentencing hearing at which Crisp, the Defence counsel, seemed vague even on the timing of the incident, until the Prosecutor put him right. Of course, his knowledge of the incident was scant, he'd told the Judge, because he didn't have any of the documents.

'Why didn't you have any of the documents?' For a period I entertained a courtroom fantasy— Crisp, entrapped in the witness box, squirms under my cross-examination. 'Did you ask the Prosecution for the documents? Had you not asked your client how the police came by his DNA in the first place? Perhaps you preferred to be ignorant of your client's past dealing with police? Maybe you thought it better not to know too much, to hear no evil? If you did ask your client, do you recall if his family members were present? I put it to you that as a prudent barrister you should have, ought to have, might reasonably have had cause to …'

Yes, he should have. But he didn't. And what about Slim, the Prosecutor? What's his defence? He was aware that the incident had happened the night before Maria's alleged rape, but neither he, nor his instructors in the OPP, thought it necessary to check out the police file and learn more details. What could possibly explain the complete absence of prudence, or even of nosiness, about the true character of the young man he was paid to argue should be locked up? Didn't he want to take the measure of the man in the dock?

No matter how many times my mind chased these questions it always crashed into the same conclusion: the Prosecutor believed he knew all he needed to know about a man such as Jama.

⋈

Slim had declined to speak with me. While the OPP was happy to facilitate my meeting with Sonnet so I could learn the good part of the story, the part that reflected well on the Crown, it blocked any attempt for me to make sense of the dark chapter that came before. The OPP refused to answer a list of questions about the proceedings against Jama. A spokeswoman told me its role had been '… thoroughly analysed' in the Vincent inquiry. We have nothing more to add'.

In contrast to the Crown's stony silence, I eventually got the chance, in a series of phone calls, to interview Crisp. The righteous indignation that had inspired my courtroom fantasy subsided once I sensed the heaviness in his voice. We spoke in short bursts. He was either on a bus in Sydney or in a conference with clients, or tied up in court. I floated my theory that Jama had been nervous to offer up details about the pool hall incident, especially as his parents were often on the scene.

'He came from a deeply religious, deeply conservative background,' I said.

Crisp remembered the family, particularly the father. They were a supportive family, 'pleasant, interested, concerned'. He couldn't, however, reveal anything Jama had told him or not told him—these were confidential discussions between lawyer and client. But on the subject of the night before, I really must understand that he had no access to any of the documents and so couldn't possibly have discovered the Austin hospital link between the two women.

I asked why he decided not to put Jama in the witness box to give his own alibi evidence; a clumsy chorus of witnesses insisted Jama was home all night, and not a word from the man himself? There was a recording of Jama's interview with police, Crisp responded, and in such cases the jury can hear the accused's complete and contemporaneous version of events without the need for him to be cross-examined. He came to the view that Jama ought to be spared from cross-examination by the Crown. The decision about whether to put one's client in the box is always a tricky judgment call, it's a process of weighing everything up—the evidence, his impression of the accused …

'*Did you think he was guilty?*' I asked.

'No. Absolutely not. I absolutely reject that.'

'But otherwise none of it makes sense,' I persisted. 'I mean, it wasn't just that there was no evidence linking Jama to the nightclub, but in fact all the evidence indicated precisely the opposite, that he wasn't there at all. No one saw a black man, there were no phone records to put him there, he didn't appear on the security footage—'

'No fingerprints in the toilets,' Crisp chimed in, momentarily dropping his guard.

'No fingerprints in the toilets. So if everything, everything, points to his innocence except the DNA evidence, then as a matter of logic you have to conclude that, well, that evidence is somehow wrong. It must be wrong. And by that I don't mean the science is wrong, but that the basic assumption suggested in the evidence is wrong. But you didn't do that. You didn't question the assumption that because his sperm was found on the slide and the swab, he had to be guilty. The only way I can explain that is you assumed he was guilty. Not just you, but all of you, all the lawyers in that courtroom.'

'I reject that,' Crisp repeated, his tone surprisingly unflustered.

The Prosecution, he said, probably thought Jama was guilty. But as a Defence barrister he wouldn't represent someone he thought was guilty. Most of the time he wouldn't, he wouldn't want to …

Crisp petered out and then recharged.

'As a Defence barrister you always keep an open mind. You have to. And I can tell you in this case, I myself, and my instructors, we all had an open mind.'

Prior to these exchanges with Crisp I had assumed that at the very least a subconscious belief in his client's guilt had shaped his thinking through the trial. But his insistence that he'd kept an 'open mind' about Jama's culpability made me wonder if I'd entirely misread him. Crisp had accepted the Prosecution's assurance that the DNA sample was unlikely to have been contaminated in the police laboratory. The possibility that contamination might have occurred *before* the sample's arrival at the lab, simply hadn't occurred to Crisp or to anyone else.

So it is true Crisp did not question the basic, and tragically wrong, assumption in the DNA evidence. He instead proffered alternative theories, including that a man other than Jama had had sex with Maria either at the nightclub or in the preceding days. He suggested to forensic biologist Deborah Scott that sperm could survive several days in a woman's cervix. He tried to allege the DNA analysis of Maria's swab contained traces of a 'third person'. I also remembered how, at the committal, Crisp latched onto the theme of Maria's underwear, or lack thereof, at the nightclub.

And it struck me that perhaps Crisp's accepting the DNA evidence at face value stemmed from preconceptions about Maria, a woman with troubles in her personal life. Might he have perceived her as vulnerable and erratic? Perhaps, quite apart from any doubts he may have had about the accused, he couldn't shake his assumptions about the victim. Perhaps Crisp was so sure that Maria, despite her assertions to the contrary, had a habit of reckless, dissociative sex, that his mind was firmly shut to the possibility that the forensic evidence could be the result of totally innocent human error.

Chapter 25

Then came the audits of crisis care units, working groups on this and that, interim practice arrangements for the provision of forensic medical examinations.

'Furnishings, in particular, chairs/couches, to be made of impermeable material that can be easily wiped clean.'
'Equipment and materials required: single-use sachets of lubricating jelly.'
'Using Det-Sol 500 cleaning fluid and a disposable wipe … wipe down any other non-disposable equipment you have used—phone, light source; sphygmomanometer, auroscope …'

The case had shed light on numerous problems; crucial problems, the professionals assured me, such as the still unresolved turf war between the Institute of Forensic Medicine and the Centres Against Sexual Assault as to which body ought to control the fifteen crisis care units scattered across Victoria.

Each of the CASAs is a separate organisation that's either connected to a large hospital or is a community-based agency with its own Board of Management. The hospital-based CASA units were supposed to be cleaned by the same staff who attend to operating theatres and other rooms, but in reality there had been protocols, of varying formality, on who cleaned the rooms and when. Or, as the Institute of Forensic Medicine would contend, who cleared away the pizza boxes after the orderlies were done socialising. And even though the forensic doctors have since switched to sealed rape kits, even if they lock up their equipment, even if they now assume responsibility themselves for cleaning the examination room, there's still only so much the Institute can control.

Even in the time since the Jama scandal, for instance, the Institute has had to force the closure of the CASA crisis care unit at Sunshine hospital for three weeks, after finding dirt in the sink and dust on the ledges. The unit is only used about once a fortnight, the Institute says, and it's the same with many others.

So the Institute argues for getting rid of most of these units, and handing it control over one or two 'centres of forensic excellence'. The Institute questions whether an advocacy group should enjoy so privileged a position in our criminal justice system. (Vincent doesn't think so, and said as much in his report.) As someone from the Institute explained, rape counsellors would still remain on the scene to deliver victims critical advice, 'a cup of tea and a pair of trackies'. Surely, the argument goes, rape victims deserve an assurance that the forensic evidence in their case will be handled with the utmost professionalism and surely for the sake of that assurance they'd be prepared to travel further to a medical examination.

The 'centres of forensic excellence' model works for London so why wouldn't it also work for Melbourne? Because Melbourne is much larger than London, respond the counsellors of CASA, through their manager Carolyn Worth, a woman with a shock of blonde hair, who speaks in a soothing purr. Worth points out that the counsellors in the south-east region, where she herself is based, are spread from Portsea to Port Melbourne and down to Pakenham. As it is, a person who is raped in Sorrento has to travel at least an hour to get to Clayton. Force the victims to travel even further, and they may opt not to report the crime at all.

Worth is a veteran of Melbourne's inaugural women's-only Reclaim the Night march and of the Women's Liberation Halfway House Collective, circa 1975. She remembers all too well the 'bad old days'. She says we ought to resist hysterical overreaction. The Jama scenario was basically a one-off. With proper cleaning regimes and revamped examination rooms (and proper resourcing to bring about the latter) the risk of something like this happening again is remote.

These CASA units also host an after-hours family violence service. Sometimes, if there's no forensic doctor around, the counsellors will spend hours with a rape victim. A third of the people seen in the south-east region choose not to report to the police anyway, Worth says. It is imperative the victims are made comfortable. They don't want to feel like specimens in a petri dish. Because let's face it, Worth says, even when the police do become involved, the forensic evidence is rarely critical. Most of the time, according to Worth, the sexual assault allegation comes down to he said, she said. It has always been thus.

In the end, it was a footnote in one of the reports that commanded my attention more than anything else: *'The term "patient" may be interchanged with "victim/survivor".'* Someone had clearly deemed this linguistic aside too important to omit.

I struggled to work up an interest in 'permeable surfaces'. And in the post-Jama resurrection of the Victorian chapter of the Australian Academy of Forensic Sciences, re-established to broaden the understanding of lawyers and the public generally, in matters DNA. And even in the new procedures in the police lab—including the introduction of a checklist for police investigators when DNA is the only evidence in a case.

I tried to feel galvanised at hearing that, at the time of writing, there are still no national guidelines to prevent the contamination of forensic samples, even as police gain powers to obtain DNA for a wider range of suspected offences. Or that since Jama's case an analogous instance of contamination had occurred in a crisis care unit, yes, almost the same scenario, although thankfully this time no one went to gaol because of the mishap. Worth is plainly wrong when she says the contamination in the Jama case was a one-off.

We will never live in a pristine world. Mistakes will always happen. The outrage in Jama's case was not that a mistake happened. It was that no one saw human error as the only rational explanation. As Vincent remarked in his report, the DNA evidence had cast a spell over otherwise critical minds. Reluctantly, I had come to the realisation that this spell gained its potency from the nature of the accused—a black African, a Muslim, a young man who, to borrow a phrase from the prosecutor, was not like 'most of us'. With Farah Jama in the frame, logic gave way to hypnotic suggestion. Those who condemned could only see a guilty man.

Six months after Jama's acquittal, DNA evidence in the US cleared an innocent African-American, Raymond Towler, who had spent nearly thirty years in gaol for a wrongful conviction of rape.

On YouTube, I watched the man's vindication in a packed Ohio courtroom. Towler's thick beard was streaked with grey. He sat very still, looking overwhelmed but dignified.

'You're free,' said the judge, a matronly figure in spectacles. 'May the sun shine warm on your face ... May God hold you in the palm of his hand, now and forever.' Choking back tears, she stepped down from the bench to shake Towler's hand. The gallery erupted in applause.

Thirty years.

The Attorney-General Rob Hulls came under pressure to give Jama a personal apology. The youth and his lawyer were demanding no less. Hulls wanted to say sorry but Jama was pushing the state for compensation, and he had to let that process run its course. Again, it was all a little sensitive.

In truth, the state was not obliged to pay Jama a cent. According to legal doctrine, no right of action exists for wrongful conviction: Jama retained qualified counsel, and there's no law against juries getting it wrong. But as Hulls told me, he wanted to do the right thing.

In May the following year a psychologist, asked by Jama's lawyers to assess him, diagnosed the youth as suffering from depression and post-traumatic stress disorder. The psychologist noted his shaking hands, poor concentration, insomnia, short-term memory loss and frequent flashbacks of being in gaol and standing for the guilty verdict.

The deal was finally struck nearly a year after Jama's release from prison. The media reported the State Government had awarded Jama $525,000. It was an 'adequate settlement', as his lawyer told the ABC, 'provided that Mr Jama is happy and can move on with his life'.

After the legalities were sorted, Hulls, also Deputy Premier at the time, invited Jama to his office at Treasury Place. The guests had initially wanted their lawyers present, but Hulls said that wouldn't be necessary or appropriate. A couple of men accompanied Jama, one of them, presumably Osman, introducing himself as a community leader. Hulls offered an apology.

'The system let you down,' he said, 'but ultimately justice prevailed'. Jama spoke of his aspirations for the future, of the trauma he had endured.

Hulls left the meeting thinking, 'really nice kid'.

※

Jama received half a million. His lawyer had demanded five million, and I guess perfect justice would command at least that. What monetary sum could possibly compensate for the indignity and the shame, for robbing a man of almost a year and a half of his youth?

His claim was as morally sound as it was characteristically naive and misjudged. A worker who loses a limb on the factory floor would struggle to pocket anywhere near that amount. But Jama's ambit claim struck me as less a negotiating strategy than a reflection of his persistent, sometimes pathetic, tendency to misread circumstances. His template was perhaps America, the native territory of the ambulance chaser and the stratospheric payout.

The episode made me think of all the stories I had heard of Somalis getting to this end of the world by accident, thinking they were heading somewhere else. Stowaways on cargo ships, crouching among the cobwebs in the darkness, fantasising about the future, until they finally emerged, blinking and disoriented, to the glare of the southern sun.

※

Hulls ceased being Attorney-General after his party lost power in November 2010. Six months later Rapke resigned as Director of Public Prosecutions after a serious falling out with the Chief Crown Prosecutor, Silbert, and an inquiry, also conducted by Vincent, found he had made an error of judgment in his handling of the promotion of a female lawyer. A month later Police Chief Commissioner Overland resigned after a serious falling out with Jones, his former deputy, and an Ombudsman's report that criticised his decision to release incomplete crime statistics in the lead-up to the state election.

Dominoes fell, heads rolled, the climate of the times grew ever hotter.

Brett Sonnet, knee deep in gangland murders, witness to a procession of colourful and dangerous characters, continued his meteoric rise through the Prosecution. In the year that followed his involvement in the Jama case, he was appointed a full Crown Prosecutor, becoming the first solicitor in the history of the state to attain the position, normally the prize of veteran barristers. Two years after that, in a somewhat neat irony, he took over as head of the Crown's specialist Sex Offences Unit. Yet for all his rich experiences, Sonnet still nominates the Jama case as his finest, most satisfying moment. 'Best case I've done in twenty-two years,' he'll tell you. 'Best case I'll ever do.'

Nearly two years after he heard Jama's case, Judge Lacava sentenced Melbourne's notorious 'hot-chocolate rapist' to a minimum nine years' gaol for raping three women after he had spiked their drinks.

What of the other people caught up in the extraordinary chain of events? Of Maria, Vincent remarked in his report that she presumably experienced some relief from the knowledge she was never raped in the first place, 'but then had to come to terms with very different information and a dramatically altered personal situation'.

I liked his choice of words, 'dramatically altered personal situation'. Maria's experience, if she were ever to share it, would doubtless be fertile material for sociologists and social workers and psychiatrists. A woman who experienced more than three years of her life as a rape victim, only to later be told she was nothing of the sort.

What took place—or is it, what didn't take place?—at Venue 28, had the impact of a hand-grenade in Maria's life. However, in the years that followed the trial, she progressed along a path that demanded diligence and mental clarity and doggedness. Everyone confirmed that she responded to the news of the monumental bungle with abundant grace. Vincent had the strong impression that she was handling circumstances 'extremely well'.

I persisted in trying to weigh the glowing assessments of others, and the largely steady and forthright woman I had glimpsed in the court transcript, against her inexplicably reckless conduct that night in Doncaster. Each time my mind conjured the sequence of events at the nightclub it met with static interference—Maria aroused such complex and potent emotions.

Even though she and I had never set eyes on one another, both Maria's steadiness and her fragility were oddly palpable and deeply poignant. Her trauma sprang straight from an archetypal nightmare. Maria surfaces to find herself exposed in front of strangers. Her memory wiped, she's unable to account for events, helpless to bear witness. What else was she supposed to think in those first chaotic moments? Perhaps if she had awoken on the toilet floor, perhaps if 'pull up her pants' wasn't the first thing she heard on regaining consciousness, she might not have been assailed by sinister fears, and none of this would have happened. But once the thought that someone had violated her took hold she couldn't possibly shake it off. Maria simply did as any woman in her situation would do. She asked the question.

I was painfully aware of the risk that my book might bring her fresh pain and anxiety. All I could do was draw comfort from my knowledge of her forgiving and spectacularly resilient nature.

Taylah's text messages were invariably apologetic—'sorry I've taken so long getting back to you'—attesting to a life busy with motherhood, study and the quest for betterment. Every once in a while we'd chat on the phone about her life. About her uni assignments, her son, her falling out with so-and-so over such-and-such. At our only meeting, she had told of her ambition to obtain a university degree; she'd earn more money that way. And she had been 'for the last four years stable in private rental'. She giggled, 'I'm a success story.' Ideally, she'd work in homelessness or child protection, remarking 'if someone would have helped me as a kid I might not have gone through such a rocky stage'.

But she would probably need to leave town, yet again.

'People round *here* just aren't interested in improving their lives,' she had said at our meeting, tossing her plaits in her haughty, endearing way.

As for Uncle Osman, he continued to talk to journalists (with the understandable exception of this one), supplying quotes on the controversies of the day: terror laws, Sharia courts, multiculturalism and, of course, integration. I had bristled at the report, written after his outburst about police terrorists, which referred to him as having been 'until now' a voice of moderation.

I guess the journalist was trying to do Osman a good turn by including the phrase. Still, I thought, if people only knew the heroic scale of Osman's 'moderation'. How even once his nephew had been wrongly convicted he managed to express concern about the way the 'Australian population' might view a weeping mother outside a courtroom. Or how, back in March 2008, as Jama awaited trial for a crime he didn't commit, Osman responded calmly to a tabloid report that people born overseas committed one in seven crimes in Victoria, including a quarter of rapes, and that one in nine people born in Somalia committed a crime in the previous year.

Osman had assured the newspaper his community was peaceful, and working with the police to solve problems and 'misunderstandings'. At every turn, Osman impressed with his composure, his magnanimity—he ought to have been allowed one errant remark.

Lastly to Jama, whose story I hope to read one day, this book being another story altogether.

In February 2013, nearly two years after our first meeting, I made one last attempt to speak with him. I made the approach through his lawyer, Kimani Boden.

'I've got you on loudspeaker,' Boden said. 'Farah is here. He's listening.'

I explained that I would be giving my publisher a draft of the book in coming days, 'but it's still not too late for Farah to tell me his story'.

Boden said the decision was up to his client: 'If he doesn't call you back then obviously that'll mean he's not interested'.

He did not call me back.

I wondered if Jama dared go clubbing with Abdulkadir Mohamed any more and whether he still subscribed to the Islamic law prohibiting sex before marriage. Did he have any faith at all in the justice system? I was curious to know if he would describe himself as 'integrated' and whether he'd thought some more about women in this society and how much power they ought to have. Did he think anything good came out of his ordeal, and did he feel optimistic about his future?

In his *Age* interview, Jama told of how he was reluctant to go out for months after his ordeal. He would do the shopping but only if accompanied. He refused to go on a family outing to Luna Park because of the risk of crowds, teenagers and trouble, meaning the police. In the first winter following his release, he gave in to pressure from mates and went along to a Friday night footy match, Hawthorn and Essendon. The cops were everywhere. He had to hide his terror. But he got through it.

I was told that after Jama's compensation payment came through, his mother travelled overseas. She visited relatives in the region of Puntland in Somalia.

On hearing this I smiled, sharing quietly in a sweet catharsis. How wonderful that she could visit the homeland. Not the fantasyland that could have been or should have been, but the real homeland, where real people were trying to salvage from the wreckage of the past a better future.

How wonderful to go home.

I was told she also went to Saudi Arabia, for a pilgrimage to Mecca. There had been deaths in the family, a sick child, a son imprisoned and finally set free. She had some hefty accounts to settle with God, the ultimate judge, and in his courtroom, at least, she would be speaking her mind.

www.ingramcontent.com/pod-product-compliance
Lightning Source LLC
Chambersburg PA
CBHW050629300426
44112CB00012B/1721